ABOUT THE AUTHORS

Noel Harvey, B.A. Mod. (Dub.), M.A., Ph.D. (Wisc.), lectures in industrial relations and supervisory management at the National College of Industrial Relations. He is the author of *Effective Supervisory Management in Ireland* and numerous articles for international business journals. He has carried out extensive research in Ireland, the US and Germany.

Adrian Twomey, B.C.L. (N.U.I.), M.Litt. (Dub.), Barrister-at-Law, (Kings Inns), is an associate lecturer in law at the National College of Industrial Relations and a former employee of the Department of Labour. He specialises in labour and constitutional law and has published numerous articles in Irish legal journals, as well as collaborating with Noel Harvey in the writing of *Effective Supervisory Management in Ireland*.

SEXUAL HARASSMENT IN THE WORKPLACE

A PRACTICAL GUIDE FOR EMPLOYERS AND EMPLOYEES IN IRELAND

NOEL HARVEY

B.A. (Dub.), M.A., Ph.D. (Wisc.)

ADRIAN F. TWOMEY

B.C.L. (N.U.I.), M.Litt. (Dub.), Barrister-at-Law (Kings Inns)

Oak Tree Press
Dublin

Oak Tree Press
Merrion Building
Lower Merrion Street
Dublin 2, Ireland

A catalogue record of this book is
available from the British Library

ISBN 1-86076-005-8 (pbk.)

Printed in Ireland by Colour Books Ltd.

To Sandra and Peadar
(N.H.)

To Sinéad
(A.T.)

CONTENTS

FOREWORD

We have shown considerable foresight in this country in recognising early on the seriousness of the problem of sexual harassment in the workplace.

As long ago as 1985 the Labour Court interpreted the Employment Equality Act of 1977 in such a way as to ensure that many successful cases were taken by victims of this kind of harassment. At that time the Labour Court declared that "freedom from sexual harassment is a condition of work which an employee of either sex is entitled to expect".

There is no question but that there was a need for a practical guide for both employers and employees, such as this one. The authors, Dr Harvey and Mr Twomey, are to be commended not just for their initiative in producing this guide, but also for their erudition and skill in writing a manual which is both accessible and accurate in its interpretation of the law as it currently stands on this important issue.

In 1994 I requested the Employment Equality Agency to prepare a Code of Practice on the subject of sexual harassment. A text was subsequently produced which had the backing of the government, employers and trade unions. Demand for the code following its publication was phenomenal, highlighting the fact that its publication was an important landmark in recognising the seriousness of the problem.

The publication of this guide is in my view a no less important landmark, providing as it does detailed information on the practicalities of dealing with the problem from an employer's and an employee's perspective. I believe it will be of considerable help to both. More importantly, I believe that the guide will provide real help to the victims of practices which are now thankfully regarded as unacceptable in the modern workplace.

The authors of this guide deserve to be congratulated but they also deserve our thanks for producing a document which will I know play a positive part in alleviating the distress of future victims of sexual harassment and ensuring that the appropriate sanctions are taken against the perpetrators.

Every trade union official should have a copy of this guide and no personnel department should be without it. I have no doubt that it will have the circulation and the usage which it so obviously deserves.

Mervyn Taylor, TD
Minister for Equality and Law Reform
September 1995

PREFACE

Sexual harassment is only one of many problems up to which women have had to face in the workplace over the last number of years. It remains a unique problem, however, for a number of reasons. It is remarkably damaging for both victims and their employers, in that it can destroy the careers of both parties involved, lead to medical and psychological problems, and have a devastating effect on staff morale and productivity. It is also an issue in which the media would seem to have tremendous interest, often for somewhat dubious reasons.

Despite the fact that sexual harassment has been a serious problem in the workplace for hundreds of years, it is only since the mid-1970s that it has been recognised as such and tackled. Even as late as 1995 the issue has not been specifically dealt with in legislation, although it is expected that the omission in question will be rectified by the current Government.

In the context outlined above, this book aims to fulfil four primary functions. The first is to inform employers, by explaining what sexual harassment is, what an employer's legal obligations are and how the problem should be countered. The second is to fully inform individuals who are or have been sexually harassed how they can recognise and deal with such conduct. The book's third function is to outline the law on sexual harassment in Ireland in a comprehensive, if compact, manner; something which would not seem to have been attempted in this jurisdiction heretofore. Finally, it is hoped that the book will act as a handbook on sexual harassment for trade union officials who have to deal with the issue.

In order to minimise the use of the somewhat clumsy phrases "he or she" and "him or her" victims of sexual harassment are, throughout the book, referred to as "she" while harassers are referred to as "he", on the basis that the overwhelming majority of sexual harassment cases involve male harassers and female victims.

While we are jointly responsible for the contents of the book, Noel Harvey assumed primary responsibility for Chapters Four, Five and Six and Adrian Twomey for Chapters Two, Three and Seven. Chapter One was collaborative.

We are indebted to a number of people for their helpful (and often constructively critical) comments, practical advice, support and encouragement. In particular, we would like to thank Mervyn Taylor, TD, Minister for Equality and Law Reform, who not only kindly agreed to write the foreword, but also gave us permission to include his Department's Code of Practice on sexual harassment as an appendix. His contribution is very greatly appreciated by both the authors. Sincere thanks are also due to Siobhán Butler, who agreed to allow us to reprint in Chapter Seven an article which first appeared in the *Evening Press*.

We would also like to thank Carmel Foley, Kathleen Connolly, Bernadette Forde and the other staff of the Employment Equality Agency; Máirtín de Búrca, Donal Costello, Anne Doyle, Noreen Walsh, Catherine Sheridan and all the staff in the Law Reform Division of the Department of Equality and Law Reform; Caroline Fennell, UCC Law Department; Paul Ennis, ESB; Margaret Nolan, ICTU; Peter Flood, IBEC; and all our colleagues in the National College of Industrial Relations, in particular Professor Joyce O'Connor, Catherine Corcoran and Catherine Clarke.

David Givens and his staff at Oak Tree Press were not only extremely patient and understanding, but also made a tremendous contribution in focusing and tightening up what was, initially, a rather rambling text in places. Their absolute professionalism made our task far easier.

Adrian Twomey would like to thank, in particular, his parents, Ann and Noel Twomey, and sister Denise, for their constant encouragement and support, and Sinéad for her unfailing enthusiasm, help and invaluable advice. Without her, this book would never have been completed.

Noel Harvey would like to thank his wife Sandra and son Peadar for their endless support and love.

CHAPTER ONE

WHAT IS SEXUAL HARASSMENT?

Men and women differ as to their perception of what constitutes sexual harassment. It is an issue that treads on the very explosive ground of sexual politics and the dynamics of the workplace and, let's face it, women are relative newcomers to the marketplace. It was fashioned by and for men."[1]

DEFINING SEXUAL HARASSMENT

Sexual harassment has, perhaps more than any other issue affecting modern working women, been the subject of considerable debate in the media, in workplaces and at trade union meetings over the last ten years. That debate has been prompted by a series of court cases, fuelled by the US Senate hearings concerning George Bush's nomination of Clarence Thomas for a seat on the Supreme Court bench and, most recently, exacerbated by the release of a film based on Michael Crichton's bestselling novel, *Disclosure*.[2] For that reason, the vast majority of both employers and employees have some idea of what the term "sexual harassment" means. It is, for example, generally accepted that repeatedly touching or grabbing at a colleague is unacceptable behaviour. Similarly, most employees accept that they must show some restraint in commenting on their colleagues' looks, dress sense and private lives.

The term "sexual harassment", however, remains notoriously difficult to define. As the Minister for Equality and Law Reform, Meryvn Taylor, TD, has pointed out, "[t]here is no universally ac-

---

[1] Caroline Fennell, "Sexual Harassment — A Need for Change ?", *The Irish Times*, 13 February 1989.

[2] Michael Crichton, *Disclosure* (New York: Ballantine Books, 1993).

cepted definition of sexual harassment and there are different views about where the boundaries lie."[3] What one person regards as sexual harassment may not, therefore, be considered to be harassment by another. Similarly, an individual may tolerate or even welcome comments or actions from one person, but resent to the point of complaining about the same comments or actions from somebody else. Further complicating the situation is the fact that men and women tend to have very different perspectives on the issue of sexual harassment. This gender division makes it even more difficult to arrive at a generally acceptable definition of the term "sexual harassment".

While it is almost impossible to frame a definition which will find favour with everyone, it is essential that employers and employees attempt to agree on one. In that context, it is submitted that "sexual harassment" is best defined as discriminatory behaviour which is sexual in nature as well as unwelcomed and unreciprocated by the victim.[4] It encompasses a wide range of behaviour which can include, among other things, unwelcome sexual advances, ranging from touching and propositions for sexual favours, to sexual assault and rape; verbal comments about individuals' appearances; or the open display of pornographic material.

There are, however, a number of other definitions of "sexual harassment" with which it is worth being familiar. The European Commission, for example, defines sexual harassment in very broad terms, stating that "sexual harassment means unwanted conduct of a sexual nature, or other conduct based on sex affecting the dignity of women and men at work".[5] The definition used by the Irish Employment Equality Agency[6] is more open-ended in

---

[3] Mervyn Taylor, TD, Minister for Equality and Law Reform, in his address to the Irish Nurses' Organisation at their seminar "Sexual Harassment is No Laughing Matter", Dublin, 5 May 1993.

[4] Other definitions of sexual harassment are included in Figure 1.2.

[5] Commission of the European Communities, *How to Combat Sexual Harassment at Work: A Guide to Implementing the European Commission Code of Practice* (Brussels: European Commission, 1993), at 21.

[6] The Employment Equality Agency is a statutory body, established by the Government in 1977 and charged, *inter alia*, with (a) working towards the

that the Agency does not attempt to be comprehensive, opting instead to describe sexual harassment as

> behaviour which includes unreciprocated and unwelcome comments; looks; jokes; suggestions or physical contact which might threaten a person's job security or create a stressful or intimidating working environment.[7]

The Agency's definition, while useful, is somewhat unreliable in that, unlike other definitions, it makes no reference to the sexual nature of sexual harassment. As a result, conduct such as bullying, which is not sexually motivated and is not simply aimed at women, would, under the Agency's definition, constitute sexual harassment. For that reason, it is submitted that employers and unions would be wiser to use an alternative, and more comprehensive, definition.

Conduct Encompassed by the Definition

Despite disagreements between individuals and organisations about how one can best define sexual harassment, there is broad consensus in respect of the kinds of activities which should come within the scope of any definition. That consensus is reflected in the Department of Equality and Law Reform's *Code of Practice,*[8] which classifies sexual harassment into three categories: verbal, physical and non-verbal or visual harassment (see Figure 1.1).

Similarly, the British TUC has opined that

> a broad definition of sexual harassment would include repeated and unwanted verbal or sexual advances, sexually explicit derogatory statements or sexually discriminatory remarks which

---

elimination of discrimination in relation to employment, and (b) promoting equality of opportunity between men and women in relation to employment. See sections 34 *et seq.* of the Employment Equality Act, 1977.

[7] Employment Equality Agency, *Equality at Work: A Model Equal Opportunities Policy,* (Dublin, 1991), at 61. Emphasis added. The Minister for Equality and Law Reform, Mervyn Taylor, TD, has added that "any conduct which causes a person to be conscious of their sex role over their work role is a form of sexual harassment."

[8] Department of Equality and Law Reform, *Code of Practice: Measures to Protect the Dignity of Women and Men at Work,* (Dublin, 1994). The text of the Code is reproduced as Appendix I.

are offensive to the worker involved, which cause the worker to feel threatened, humiliated, patronised or harassed or which interfere with the worker's job performance, undermine job security or create a threatening or intimidating work environment. Sexual harassment can take many forms, from leering, ridicule, embarrassing remarks or jokes, unwelcome comments about dress or appearance, deliberate abuse, the repeated and/or unwanted physical contact, demands for sexual favours, or physical assaults on workers."[9]

Figure 1.1: Code of Practice — Classes of Sexual Harassment[10]

Verbal Harassment	Physical Harassment	Non-Verbal/Visual Harassment
• Unwelcome sexual advances • Unwelcome pressure for social contact • Sexually suggestive jokes, remarks or innuendoes	• Unwelcome physical contact such as groping, pinching, patting or unnecessary touching • Unwelcome fondling or kissing • Sexual assault or rape	• Sexually suggestive or pornographic pictures and calendars • Leering, offensive gestures, whistling

All-encompassing definitions of sexual harassment, such as that used by the TUC, should not, however, be taken to preclude individuals from becoming romantically involved with co-workers. Asking a co-worker for a date is not, in and of itself, an act of sexual harassment. The law does not in any sense interfere with relationships between people providing those relationships are based on consensus. For additional definitions of sexual harassment see Figure 1.2.

---

[9] Trades Union Congress, *Guidelines*; as quoted in Nathalie Hadjifotiou, *Women and Harassment at Work*, (London: Pluto Press, 1983), at 8.

[10] *Code of Practice, op cit.*, at 9-10.

Figure 1.2: Definitions of Sexual Harassment

Sexual Harassment is "[b]ehaviour which includes unreciprocated and unwelcome comments; looks; jokes; suggestions or physical contact which might threaten a person's job security or create a stressful or intimidating working environment." — Employment Equality Agency, A Model Sexual Harassment Policy, Dublin, 1991.

"Sexual Harassment means unwanted conduct of a sexual nature, or other conduct based on sex affecting the dignity of women and men at work. This can include unwelcome physical, verbal or non-verbal conduct." — Commission of the European Communities, Code of Practice.

"Sexual Harassment is unsolicited, unreciprocated behaviour of a sexual nature to which the recipient objects or could not reasonably be expected to consent and may include: unwanted physical contact; lewd or suggestive behaviour, whether verbal or physical; sexually derogatory statements or sexually discriminatory remarks; the display of pornographic or sexually explicit material in the workplace." — Public Service Executive Union/Department of Finance.

"Sexual Harassment at work is any conduct of a sexual nature unwanted by the recipient and which infringes on her dignity as a person. It includes, for instance, physical contact and invasion of personal space, comments of a sexual nature, displaying pornographic images and making sexual propositions. Sexual Harassment can be expressed verbally, in deeds, gestures or other sexually charged behaviour." — German Ministry of Women and Youth.

"Sexual Harassment is any sexually oriented practice that endangers an individual's continued employment, negatively affects his/her work performance, or undermines his/her sense of personal dignity." — Arjun P. Aggarwal, *Sexual Harassment in the Workplace*, 2nd ed., Canada, 1992.

Sexual Harassment is "any conduct, comment, gesture or contact of a sexual nature (a) that is likely to cause offence or humiliation to any employee; or (b) that might, on reasonable grounds, be perceived by that employee as placing a condition of a sexual nature on employment or on any opportunity for training or promotion." — Canada Labour Code, R.S.C. 1985, c. 9 (1st Supp.), s.17.

Why Women are Sexually Harassed
Over the last ten to fifteen years a considerable number of aca-
demics and industrial relations practitioners have expounded
theories which attempt to explain why women are sexually harassed in the workplace. As Hadjfotiou observes, however,

> sexual harassment at work . . . cannot be explained away as the
> sudden aberration of particular men with psychological problems
> or strange perversions. Behaviour at work is, in fact, similar to
> that elsewhere. Women are frequently whistled and shouted at
> in the street, manhandled in buses and trains, chatted up in
> pubs, and sexually abused in their own homes.[11]

Workplace sexual harassment, therefore, is not unlike many of
the other forms of discrimination against women which pervade
modern society, in that it is a product of the sexist socialisation
and stereotyping which begins to influence the attitudes and actions of individuals from an early age. The problem has been
highlighted by Helena Kennedy, who explains that:

> Even as a child it seemed to me that if there was one body of
> people who were tougher on women than on men it was other
> women, a puzzling contradiction given the strength of the female
> bonds in my community. However, for the most part I just ac-
> cepted that there were higher expectations of women.... Men
> were simply victims of their own appetites, hardly capable of free
> will when it came to sex or violence, and it was up to us to act as
> the restraining influence. After all, woman was responsible for
> the original sin. It was only later that I came to the conclusion
> that Eve had been framed.
>
> I swallowed the idea that women should generally be expected
> to behave better than men, since there seemed ample evidence
> that they did so anyway, and I could see no harm in keeping up
> the standard. However, my sense of natural justice balked at the
> idea of holding women responsible for male transgressions....
> Transportation from Paradise is one thing, but a sentence of
> eternal damnation when the conviction had to be based on the
> uncorroborated testimony of a co-accused must surely constitute

---

[11] Hadjifotiou, *op. cit.*, 23.

a breach of international standards on human rights. Poor old Eve.[12]

Kennedy's description of her girlhood beliefs might equally have been written by many Irish women, for Ireland is, in the words of the Second Commission on the Status of Women, "at the more sexist end of the EC scale".[13] To illustrate their point the Commission included in their *Report to Government*[14] the results of a European Commission survey which would seem to suggest that Irish attitudes to working women were the most sexist in Europe (see Figure 1.3). Respondents were asked whether they would be as confident in a woman performing particular services for them as they would be in a man. While 86 per cent of Danish respondents stated, for example, that they would have as much confidence in a female bus driver as in a male driver, only 43 per cent of Irish respondents answered in kind. The results of the survey, while disturbing, go some way towards explaining why women are on the receiving end of a broad range of discriminatory practices in Irish workplaces.

The problem is compounded by the fact that female workers are concentrated in the lower grades in many places of employment. As the Irish Congress of Trade Unions (ICTU) have pointed out,

> [w]omen constitute 76 per cent of all clerical workers, 57 per cent of shop assistants, 55 per cent of service workers and 51 per cent of professional and technical workers, but only 12 per cent of administrative, executive and managerial workers.[15]

Large numbers of women, therefore, find themselves working for male supervisors. Those supervisors clearly have a degree of con-

---

[12] Helena Kennedy, *Eve was Framed: Women and British Justice*, (London: Vintage, 1992), 17-18.

[13] Second Commission on the Status of Women, *Report to Government*, (Dublin, 1993), 97.

[14] *Op. cit.*

[15] ICTU, *Positive Action for Equal Opportunities at Work: Guidelines for Negotiators* (Dublin: ICTU, undated), 1.

trol over female employees which enables them to harass their subordinates more easily. As MacKinnon explains:

> [w]omen employed in the paid labor force, typically hired "as women," dependent upon their income and lacking job alternatives, are particularly vulnerable to intimate violation in the form of sexual abuse at work.[16]

Figure 1.3: Percentage of Individuals Having Equal Confidence in Both Sexes for Various Occupations

Country	Bus/train driver	Surgeon	Barrister	Public Rep.
Denmark	86	85	82	86
Netherlands	75	84	75	79
France	77	70	70	68
UK	61	70	66	75
Belgium	67	66	64	67
Spain	56	65	69	67
Portugal	52	67	65	63
W. Germany	57	55	59	64
Luxembourg	47	58	60	62
Greece	52	56	61	58
Italy	54	56	55	59
Ireland	43	51	50	61

Also exacerbating the problem is the fact that women have, in recent years, been obtaining employment in fields traditionally dominated by men. According to IBEC, the concurrent refusal by men to accept the presence of women in their previously all-male work environments is one of the main reasons why women are sexually harassed.[17]

---

[16] Catharine A. MacKinnon, *Sexual Harassment of Working Women: A Case of Sex Discrimination*, (New Haven and London: Yale University Press, 1979), 1.

[17] IBEC, *Guidelines for Employers*, (Dublin: IBEC, 1990).

Debunking the "Power" Myth

As has already been pointed out, sexual harassment is best defined as discriminatory behaviour which is *sexual in nature* as well as being unwelcome to, and unreciprocated by, the victim. There are, however, both individuals and organisations who define sexual harassment as being behaviour which is other than sexual in nature. Surprisingly, the Employment Equality Agency is one such organisation. In its 1991 *Model Policy* the Agency stated that:

> Sexual harassment has little to do with sexual attraction. It is an abuse of power. Because of this, it is usually women who are harassed, as they are mainly in the lower paid and graded positions and men in the positions of power. However, there are no stereotypical victims. Women in quite high positions in organisations can have this weapon of power wielded against them to "put them in their place".[18]

The Agency would appear to have confused sexual harassment, or unwanted and unreciprocated sexual conduct, with gender-based harassment. The distinction between the two is very fine, but is, equally, of crucial importance, for harassment which occurs because the harasser occupies a position of power, but is not sexually motivated, is harassment of a quite different nature to that which the Agency purports to be attempting to combat. It does not include persistent requests for dates, or sexual assault. Rather, it encompasses a spectrum of activity which ranges from simply annoying subordinates to bullying them.

It is arguable that the Agency's apparent confusion is caused by the fact that the majority of sexual harassment cases involve harassment of subordinates by staff in supervisory or management positions. That is not, however, to say that all, or even a large majority, of cases of sexual harassment involve such scenarios. Every case of sexual harassment where the discriminatory conduct is carried out by a co-worker or by a subordinate serves to discredit the Agency's theory. Even this point, however, would not appear to have been grasped. Rather, the Agency would seem to argue that even where a subordinate male harasses a woman in a

---

[18] Employment Equality Agency, *Model Policy, op. cit.*, at 59.

management position, the act of harassment is motivated by power rather than by any sexual motivation. The power in such instances, it is argued, is that inherently attaching to the man's gender. The harasser's aim, it is suggested, is to "put" women "in their places". Such an argument would appear to lack any real credibility. At best, it gives, women in management positions little credit in terms of their ability to assert their authority and discipline staff, while, at worst, it arguably subscribes to some sort of theory of men's inherent ability to dominate women.

If the issue of "power" is of real relevance it is not because sexual harassment is more an abuse of power than activity which is sexual in nature. Rather, as the Law Society of British Columbia as pointed out, sexual harassment "transforms a working relationship of equality between people into a sexualised context in which women are systematically disempowered and thereby reinforces an inferior position for women".[19]

How Widespread is Sexual Harassment?

Canadian academic Arjun Aggarwal has claimed that "sexual harassment is one of the most serious and widespread problems facing women in employment today."[20] His view is backed up by a number of surveys in various countries.[21] As far back as 1976, for example, the American *Redbook Magazine* concluded that nine out of ten working women in America had, at some stage in their careers, been victims of sexual harassment.[22] In the UK, the Alfred Marks Bureau, an employment agency, found that 47 per cent of women and 14 per cent of men using the agency had experienced sexual harassment.[23] (See also Figure 1.4.)

---

[19] Law Society of British Colombia, *Sexual harassment in the profession: a conduct review*, (1993); as quoted in Barbara Hewson, "A recent problem?" *New Law Journal* 626, at 627.

[20] Arjun P. Aggarwal, *Sexual Harassment in the Workplace*, 2nd ed., (Toronto: Butterworths, 1992), at 2.

[21] See generally, Hadjifotiou, *op. cit.*, at 9-10.

[22] Over 9,000 women took part in the magazine's survey.

[23] See Hadjifotiou, *op. cit.*

More recently, the *Independent on Sunday* reported that one in six working women in Britain have experienced sexual harassment in their offices, shops or factories,[24] while a subsequent MORI poll[25] found that the figure was even higher, pitching it at one in three. Despite the fact that there is little consistency in the results of such polls, the one clear conclusion from even a cursory consideration of their results is that workplace sexual harassment is a major problem for working women. It would seem that such has always been the case. Over 100 years ago, Engels observed that:

> The employer is sovereign over the persons and charms of his employees. The threat of discharge suffices in nine cases out of ten. . . . . If the master is mean enough . . . his mill is also his harem; the fact that not all manufacturers use their power does not in the least change the position of the girls.[26]

Despite the many significant changes which have taken place in workplaces since Engels made his observation, sexual harassment has continued to be a real problem. As women have moved into new areas of work, the problem of sexual harassment has followed them. No profession is devoid of harassment. In England, for example, the Chairman of the Bar Council, Robert Seabrook, QC, told a meeting organised by the Young Barristers' Committee in 1994 that the problems of racial and sexual harassment at the English Bar are "urgent".[27]

---

[24] "One in six women sexually harassed", *The Independent on Sunday*, 20 October 1991.

[25] The MORI poll was conducted in 1993.

[26] Frederick Engels, *The Condition of the Working Class in England*, (London, 1892); as quoted in Hadjifotiou, *op. cit.*, at 7.

[27] "Young Bar calls for action on harassment" (1994) *New Law Journal* 1057. A year later, the Chairwoman of the Association of Women Barristers observed that "sexual harassment is still unacceptably prevalent in our profession." See Hewson, *loc. cit.* See also, "*Droit de* senior partner" (1995) *New Law Journal* 621; Nigel Pascoe, "Beyond a joke?" (1995) *New Law Journal* 665; Martin Mears, "Bigotry, cant and humbug" (1995) *New Law Journal* 624; and "Harassment Continued" (1995) *New Law Journal* 678.

Figure 1.4: Research on the Extent of Workplace Sexual Harassment

"A study carried out by the Leeds Trade Union and Community Resource and Information Centre in England found that 96% of the women in "non-traditional" women's occupations surveyed had experienced harassment."- Commission of the European Communities, *How to Combat Sexual Harassment at Work*, Brussels, 1993.

"Out of all French men and women aged 18 and above, 21% had first-hand experience of harassment and 9% of working women have experienced highly or moderately unpleasant situations. A further 6% of women have witnessed harassment. Also, 6% of men have witnessed harassment."- Louis Harris poll, France.

"In 1988, [a survey] by the U.S. Merit Systems Protection Board concluded that some 36,000 employees in the U.S. Federal Government quit their job[s] because of sexual harassment during a two year period between 1985 and 1987."- Arjun P. Aggarwal, *Sexual Harassment in the Workplace*, 2nd ed., Canada, 1993.

"The Shapland Report surveyed 822 English law students on the 1989-90 Bar Finals course through pupillage and into practice. It found that 40% of the women surveyed had experienced sexual harassment; 10% of them experiencing harassment of an extremely serious nature."- Barbara Hewson, "A recent problem ?", (1995) *New Law Journal* 626, at 626.

"A Canadian Study, Women in the Legal Profession, found that 68.2% of female lawyers in that jurisdiction had experienced or had observed other female lawyers subjected to unwanted teasing, jokes or comments of a sexual nature by male lawyers."- Barbara Hewson, "A recent problem ?", (1995) *New Law Journal* 626, at 627.

"65.9% of those asked claim never to have been the recipient of sexual harassment, 19.1% have seldom been so, 9.4% sometimes and 5.7% often."- Ligia Amancio & Maria Luisa Pedroso Science, Research into sexual harassment in the workplace, Portugal.

Neither is the problem unique to the Western world. In Japan a recent government survey revealed that more than a quarter of working women have experienced sexual harassment at work.[28]

Unfortunately, Ireland is no different. Despite claims to the contrary by many employers, it would appear, in the words of the Employment Equality Agency, that "sexual harassment is a serious and extensive problem in Ireland."[29] In 1993, a Lansdowne Market Research survey,[30] commissioned by and reported in the *Sunday Press*, found that a considerable number of Irish women have been sexually harassed (see Figure 1.5.). The *Sunday Press* survey was particularly interesting in that it involved an analysis, not only of the kinds of harassment experienced by Irish working women, but also of their opinions as to whether or not the activity involved actually constituted sexual harassment. The survey clearly revealed that many working women were ill-informed as to what sexual harassment is, given that a remarkable 46 per cent did not regard being "grabbed" by men as constituting harassment.

The reason for this failure to recognise sexual harassment is, perhaps, best explained by Rosemary Pringle, who has highlighted the fact that many women become so used to being the victims of discriminatory behaviour that they regard it as being normal:

> One day we're talking about sexual harassment and she said, "I've never been sexually harassed." And I said, "Yes you have. It's just that you're so used to it ... you don't even notice it ... you just consider that normal. You've never been treated any other way except as a sex object to the opposite sex so you don't even think about it," and she doesn't.[31]

---

[28] Kerry Hawkins, "Taking Action on Harassment", *Personnel Management*, March, 1994.

[29] Employment Equality Agency, *Model Policy, op. cit.*, at 58.

[30] The survey was conducted among a representative sample of 504 adults, aged between 23 and 33 years. The accuracy level is estimated to be plus or minus 4 per cent.

[31] Rosemary Pringle, *Secretaries Talk: Sexuality, Power and Work* (London and New York: Verso, 1989), 262.

Figure 1.5: The Sunday Press Survey on Sexual Harassment

Conduct Endured by Women	Percentage of Women Who Experienced the Kind of Conduct in Question	Percentage of Women Who Consider the Kind of Conduct in Question as Constituting Sexual Harassment
Touched/Brushed against	14	63
Unwanted demand for sex or dates	7	63
Grabbed	7	54
Stared/Leered at by men	11	28
Exposed to pin-ups	7	17
Told sexual jokes/remarks	12	16

The Costs of Sexual Harassment

The spectrum of activities which constitute sexual harassment spans an extremely wide range, running from joking, teasing and whistling at one end to touching, grabbing, sexual assault and rape at the other. Despite the extremes involved, each of these forms of sexual harassment can produce the same effects, albeit in different degrees. As the Minister for Equality and Law Reform, Meryvn Taylor, TD, has pointed out, sexual harassment:

> can be one of the most upsetting and humiliating experiences a person can suffer. It can seriously affect an employee's confidence, physical and mental health. It can be totally devastating both personally and professionally.[32]

---

[32] Mervyn Taylor, TD, *op. cit.*

Even less serious forms of sexual harassment can be extremely damaging to the victim if repeated regularly over a period of time. As Hadjifotiou points out:

> [t]he long-term damage to the health and personal well-being of people affected by work-related stress is well documented.

She goes on to list typical problems experienced by victims of sexual harassment:

- decrease in job performance and job satisfaction
- absenteeism
- anxiety, tension, irritation, depression
- increased alcohol, cigarette and drug use
- sleeplessness and tiredness
- problems with weight and diet
- migraine
- coronary heart disease
- difficulties with family and personal relationships
- physical and mental illness.[33]

Given that victims of harassment tend to suffer from the problems identified by Hadjifotiou, it is not surprising that they do not reach their full potential in work. Many victims attempt to keep away from the workplace, or parts of it, in order to avoid harassment. They take extended periods of annual leave, ring in sick or ask for transfers. Eventually, they will either resign from their positions or attempt to live with, or ignore, the problem. A woman who takes the latter option often find that there is little support available in the workplace. Few employers have policies in place and trade unions with a few exceptions have been slow to tackle the problem.

The victims of sexual harassment are not, however, the only ones to suffer. There is general consensus that sexual harassment is also a disaster for employers (see Figure 1.6). The morale of an entire workforce can suffer and productivity inevitably declines as a result. Staff tend to divide into two camps, with some defending the harasser and others supporting the victim. If the case goes to the Labour Court the employer may incur substantial legal costs

---

[33] Hadjifotiou, *op. cit.*, at 20.

and may also have to pay compensation to the victim. The harasser may be dismissed or transferred, and replacement staff have to be trained. In addition, because of the nature of sexual harassment cases, media attention is almost guaranteed and the adverse publicity which can ensue will, almost certainly, be extremely damaging to the company.

Figure 1.6: The Cost of Sexual Harassment for Employers

In 1988 the US Merit Systems Protection Board estimated that sexual harassment cost the US Federal Government $267,000,000 in paying sick leave to federal employees who missed work because of harassment, in replacing employees who left their jobs and in reduced productivity. — Aggarwal, *op. cit.*, at 3.

Twenty-four per cent of harassed women use leave time in order to avoid the situation. Approximately 15 per cent resign and 50 per cent try to ignore it. Among that 50 per cent, productivity typically decreases by about 10 per cent. — Ronni Sandroff, "Sexual Harassment in the Fortune 500", *Working Woman*, December, 1988.

In 1988 *Working Woman* magazine estimated that sexual harassment cost a typical American Fortune 500 company $6,700,000 per annum in absenteeism, employee turnover, low morale and low productivity.

Conclusion

Given that sexual harassment is a very widespread problem and that it leads to significant damage being done to the lives of many of the individuals involved, as well as to the businesses of their employers, it becomes clear why both preventative and remedial action is necessary. Such action needs to be taken by a number of parties. Employers need to implement workplace policies on sexual harassment,[34] as well as establishing appropriate complaints or grievance procedures;[35] trade unions need to educate their

---

[34] *Cf.* Chapter 4.

[35] *Cf.* Chapter 5.

members and negotiate policies with employers;[36] the state is obliged both to legislate on the matter and to provide the necessary fora for resolving disputes;[37] and individuals need to both respect the rights of others and zealously guard their own. The remaining chapters outline how those potential minefields can best be negotiated by the various parties mentioned above. In addressing the problem, however, they should bear in mind the points already highlighted in this chapter.

---

[36] *Cf.* Chapter 6.

[37] *Cf.* Chapters 2,3, and 7.

CHAPTER TWO

SEXUAL HARASSMENT AND THE LAW

Perhaps the most important lesson is that the mountain can be moved. When we started, there was absolutely no judicial precedent for allowing a sex discrimination suit for sexual harassment. Sometimes even the law does something for the first time.[1]

INTRODUCTION

The intrusion of the law into the workplace, and its regulation of the contractual relationship between employers and employees, has traditionally been the cause of some controversy. If anything, its intrusion into the realm of private morality and sexual matters has been even more controversial.[2] In the last ten years, however, legal developments have resulted in the law regulating that area of human activity in which employment and conduct of a sexual nature coincide. The result of this legal regulation of what was previously a largely unregulated sphere of human activity has been phenomenally controversial and the subject of intense debate, both in the media and in the workplace.

As English lawyer Gillian Howard has pointed out, romantic involvements "between employees [are] not uncommon. According to statistics, over 50 per cent of us will meet our marriage part-

---

[1] Catharine MacKinnon, *Feminism Unmodified: Discourses on Life and Law* (Cambridge: Harvard University Press, 1987), 116.

[2] Consider, for example, the heated debates which followed the Supreme Court's decisions in *McGee v. Attorney General*, [1974] I.R. 284, *Norris v. Ireland*, [1984] I.R. 36, and *Attorney General v. X and others*, [1992] 1 I.R. 1. The first of those cases concerned the legality of a married couple importing artificial contraceptives; the second concerned the constitutionality of statutory prohibition of homosexual activity between consenting adults; while the third case arose as a result of the then Attorney General seeking to restrain a young girl from going to England to procure an abortion.

ners at work."[3] In that context, it is not surprising that many workers resent the idea of legal regulation of sexual activity in the workplace.[4] Such a natural reaction is, however, somewhat misguided, in that it characterises the law regulating sexual harassment as interfering, prohibitive and prudish. As has been pointed out by an American judge, sex discrimination law "should not be interpreted as reaching into sexual relationships which may arise during the course of employment, but which do not have a substantial effect on that employment."[5] Rather, the developing law on sexual harassment seeks merely to prohibit unwanted sexual conduct. It is neither intended to, nor has the effect of, prohibiting normal, everyday, or "positive" sexual conduct in the workplace. As Carmel Foley, Chief Executive of the Employment Equality Agency (EEA), has pointed out:

> What the EEA means by sexual harassment is not the mutual banter, the fun and the slagging that are part of life in most workplaces. We are not a bunch of killjoy vigilantes, ready to pounce on every innocent compliment, invitation or remark. On the contrary, we believe that such interaction helps to humanise the working day. Many a budding romance starts on the assembly line, in the canteen or at the word processor![6]

The second accusation levelled against the law relating to sexual harassment is one which is usually advanced by employers.[7] It

---

[3] Gillian Howard, "Love in the Office", (1994) *New Law Journal 1762.*

[4] The term "sexual activity" as used here refers to all activity which occurs because of the genders of the participants. For that reason, it includes quite innocuous actions and is not to be regarded as encompassing only actions which constitute sexual harassment.

[5] *Per* Finesilver D.J., *Heelan v. Johns-Manville Corp.*, 451 F. Supp. 1382 (D.C. 1978).

[6] Carmel Foley, "Why we need a Code of Practice", an address to an EEA conference on sexual harassment (Making Advances), Dublin, 15 October 1993.

[7] One must acknowledge that in Ireland the main employers' representative body, IBEC, has taken an admirable stance on sexual harassment, urging its members to take steps to prevent the occurrence of such activity, and advising them as to the steps which should be taken to ensure that such is the case.

suggests that the total cost to employers of ensuring that incidents of sexual harassment do not occur is so great as to outweigh the importance of attempting to eliminate such harassment from workplaces. This argument can, and has, been articulated in a subtle and superficially persuasive manner in the past. Its inherent sexism becomes more visible, however, when one considers it as it has been posited by Richard Posner, an eminent American jurist and the leading light of a jurisprudential school of thought known as "law and economics".[8] Posner argues that

> the social . . . consequences of sex discrimination laws are murky and not necessarily positive. In any event . . . it is important to know what . . . sex discrimination laws cost; the price tag for an increase in women's self-esteem, if known, might be thought too high.[9]

Without commenting on the fact that Posner would, by implication, appear to assume that women's rights are only worth protecting if such can be done inexpensively, one can quite confidently attack the central plank of his argument by pointing to the enormous costs arising out of sexual harassment for employers.[10] Quite apart from the costs incurred as a result of absenteeism caused by the effects or fear of sexual harassment, loss of productivity because of lower staff morale and declining sales due to adverse publicity, employers now face the prospect of significantly larger claims for damages as the European Court of Justice has, quite recently, held that there can be no statutory limit on claims for damages in sex discrimination cases.[11] It would appear that it

---

[8] For a general discussion of law and economics theory, see Bruce Carolan, "Law and Economics", (1995) 13 *Irish Law Times (n.s.) 162.*

[9] Richard Posner, "An Economic Analysis of Sex Discrimination Law", (1989) *U.C.L.R.* 1311, at 1336. For a more moderate, and less distasteful, version of the "law and economics" school's approach to analysing sexual harassment law see Marie T. Reilly, "A Paradigm for Sexual Harassment: Toward the Optimal Level of Loss", (1994) 47 *Vanderbilt Law Review* 427.

[10] *Cf.* Chapter 1.

[11] *Marshall v. Southampton and South West Hampshire Area Health Authority (Teaching), No. 2,* Case C-271/91, ECJ judgment of 2 August 1993.

is simply a matter of time before the first million pound law suit for sexual harassment reaches the courts in Ireland.

WOMEN, WORK AND THE LAW

It is generally accepted by lawyers that the law has, traditionally, been largely masculine in character in that it has, for many years, defined itself by reference to male standards and norms.[12] Labour law, or that part of the law which regulates employer-employee relationships, has also traditionally been moulded to fit such standards and norms.[13] For that reason it has often been guilty of failing to comprehend and cater for physiological differences between men and women. When it has attempted to do so, it has usually drawn distinctions between the sexes which, in the words of Mr. Justice Barton, "rested upon considerations of decorum, and upon the unfitness of certain painful and exacting duties in relation to the finer qualities of women."[14]

Despite such inglorious beginnings, Irish employment equality law has made remarkable strides since Ireland's accession to the European Economic Community in 1973.[15] In the following four years the Oireachtas passed two landmark pieces of legislation which significantly improved the legal position of women workers.[16] The first of those statutes, the Anti-Discrimination (Pay)

---

[12] See, generally, Helena Kennedy, *Eve was Framed: Women and British Justice,* (London: Vintage, 1992).

[13] See, generally, Deirdre Curtin, *Irish Employment Equality Law* (Dublin: Round Hall Press, 1985), 1-42.

[14] *Frost v. The King* [1919] I.R. 81.

[15] In his foreword to Deirdre Curtin's *Irish Employment Equality Law, op. cit.,* Judge T.F. O'Higgins of the European Court of Justice noted that "Ireland's decision to join the European Communities . . . led . . . to profound changes in the law affecting the employer/employee relationship and in particular to the giving to workers of rights of equality in pay and conditions of employment which previously would never have been thought attainable." At xv.

[16] The definitive work on Irish employment equality law, which deals comprehensively with both pieces of legislation, is Deirdre Curtin's seminal *Irish Employment Equality Law, op cit.* Despite the fact that it is now ten years

Act, 1974, as its title suggests, was intended to tackle the problem of gender-based discrimination in relation to pay. While the struggle for equal pay has not yet been successfully concluded, the passing of the 1974 Act was a significant development. As Curtin points out:

> The entry into force of the Anti-Discrimination (Pay) Act, 1974, combined with the refusal by the European Commission to permit any derogation by the Irish Government from its European Community obligations, heralded, to borrow James Connolly's terminology, the beginning of the end of the "martyrdom" of Irish women workers.[17]

The second legislative landmark referred to above was the Employment Equality Act, 1977, which made it unlawful to discriminate between individuals on grounds of sex or marital status in recruitment for employment, conditions of employment (other than remuneration or pension schemes), training or work experience, or in opportunities for promotion. While the 1977 Act was aimed primarily at eliminating discrimination by employers, it also made unlawful discrimination in activities which are related to employment, such as discrimination by organisations providing training courses, trade unions or employment agencies, as well as prohibiting the display or publication of discriminatory advertisements.

Given that such considerable progress was made in the first four years of Ireland's membership of the European Communities, it is somewhat surprising that eighteen years after the enactment of the Employment Equality Act, and ten years after the Labour Court first upheld a claim for damages for sexual harassment, such conduct is still not expressly mentioned in legislation. While it is expected that legislation dealing expressly with sexual harassment will be written into the statute book during the lifetime of the current Government, it has, at least until quite recently, been left to the Labour Court to map out the contours of sexual harassment law in this jurisdiction. In fulfilling its cartographical

---

since its publication, those who are interested in learning more about the Acts in question need go no further than Professor Curtin's book.

[17] Curtin, *op. cit.,* at 112.

role the Court would appear to have been heavily influenced by American theories on sexual harassment law. That such should have been the Irish experience is not surprising given that it was American lawyers and feminists who first named and tackled the problem.[18] Leading this assault was Catharine MacKinnon, a crusading feminist lawyer who has, in concert with Andrea Dworkin, also campaigned against the American pornography industry. Given the enormous influence which MacKinnon and American precedents have had in this and other common law jurisdictions,[19] it is almost impossible to comprehend the Irish law on the subject without first examining MacKinnon's arguments and the American judiciary's gradual acceptance of them.

SEXUAL HARASSMENT AS SEX DISCRIMINATION

The law on sexual harassment in the United States is probably more developed than in any other country in the common law world. Despite several early setbacks, feminist lawyers in America have, in the last fifteen years or so, won a string of notable victories in the courts which have resulted in the recognition and expansion of a corpus of law relating to sexual harassment. Sexual harassment is now recognised by American courts as constituting a very serious problem in the workplace and, for that rea-

---

[18] The term "sexual harassment" would appear to have first been used in the mid-1970s in, *inter alia,* the writings of the Working Women United Institute, the Alliance Against Sexual Coercion, and Carroll Brodsky. As Curtin pointed out in 1984, "the sophisticated jurisprudence which has been developed in the American courts . . . deserves the attention of any future Irish court or tribunal to consider the matter." Deirdre Curtin, "Sexual Harassment in Employment: Developing a Standard of Employer Liability", (1984) 6 *Dublin University Law Journal* (ns) 75, at 76-77.

[19] Common law legal systems are those based on the English system which places considerable emphasis on the importance of previous decisions of the courts; a rule which is technically referred to as *stare decisis.* England, Scotland, Wales, Northern Ireland, the Republic of Ireland, the United States of America, Canada, India, Australia, New Zealand, Trinidad and Tobago, South Africa and a number of other former British colonies all adhere to the common law system. While our European partners such as France, Germany and Italy have civil rather than common law systems, decisions of English, American and Australian courts, in particular, continue to influence Irish judges.

son, awards of damages against employers have skyrocketed in that jurisdiction.

Title VII of the American Civil Rights Act, 1964, prohibits sex discrimination in employment, although it does not expressly mention sexual harassment. Title VII provides that:

It shall be unlawful employment practice for an employer -

(1) to fail or refuse to hire or to discharge any individual, or otherwise to discriminate against any individual, with respect to his compensation, terms, conditions, or privileges of employment, because of such individual's race, colour, religion, sex or national origin: or

(2) to limit, segregate, or classify his employees or applicants for employment in any way which would deprive or tend to deprive any individual of employment opportunities or otherwise adversely affect his status as an employee, because of such individual's race, colour, religion, sex or national origin.

In 1974 the US federal courts heard their first sexual harassment case: *Barnes v. Train*.[20] The plaintiff in that case argued that she had been made redundant because she rebuffed her supervisor's sexual advances. The District Court was, however, unimpressed with her legal arguments and held that sexual harassment did not constitute discrimination based on sex within the meaning of Title VII. In the following two years a string of similar decisions were handed down by the American courts.[21] In *Corne v. Bausch & Lomb Inc.*,[22] for example, the Arizona District Court found that

[a]n outgrowth of holding [sexual harassment] to be actionable under Title VII would be a potential federal lawsuit every time an employee made amorous or sexually oriented advances to-

---

[20] 13 F.E.P. 123 (D.D.C. 1974); reversed *sub nom. Barnes v. Costle*, 561 F. 2d 983 (D.C. Cir. 1977).

[21] See, for example, *Corne v. Bausch & Lomb Inc.*, 390 F. Supp. 161 (D. Ariz. 1975); *Miller v. Bank of America*, 418 F. Supp. 233 (N.D. Cal. 1976); and *Tompkins v. Public Service Electric and Gas Co.*, 422 F. Supp. 533 (D. N.J. 1977); reversed *(sub nom. Tompkins II)*, 568 F. 2d 1044 (3rd Cir. 1977).

[22] *Op. cit.*

ward another. The only sure way an employer could avoid such charges would be to have employees who were asexual.[23]

A slightly more rational justification for refusing to uphold a claim of sexual harassment under Title VII was provided by the New Jersey Federal District Court in *Tomkins v. Public Service Electric and Gas Co.*[24] The Court held, in that case, that:

> Title VII was enacted in order to remove those artificial barriers to employment which are based upon unjust and long encrusted prejudice. It aims to make careers open to talents irrespective of race or sex. It is not intended to provide a federal tort remedy for what amounts to [a] physical attack motivated by sexual desire on the part of the supervisor and which happened to occur in a corporate corridor rather than in a back alley.... [S]exual harassment is neither employment related nor sex-based, but a personal injury properly pursued in state court.[25]

In 1975, however, MacKinnon began her crusade. By the late spring of that year she had drafted and circulated an erudite and highly persuasive argument which suggested that sexual harassment had to be regarded as "sex discrimination" within the meaning of Title VII. MacKinnon essentially argued that an employer directly discriminates against a woman if, by reason of her sex, he treats her less favourably than a man. Employers had already suggested that women were being ill-treated not because of their gender, but rather because of their refusal or failure to accede to sexual demands. MacKinnon's reply was that but for the woman's gender, she would not have suffered dismissal, demotion or other adverse treatment. For that reason, she argued, sexual harassment had to be regarded as discrimination based on sex.

---

[23] *Op. cit.*, at 163.

[24] *Op. cit.*

[25] As cited in Arjun P. Aggarwal, *Sexual Harassment in the Workplace*, 2nd ed., (Toronto: Butterworths,1992), at 19. In *Corne v. Bausch and Lomb Inc.*, *op. cit.*, the District Court of Arizona held that the activity of the harasser was "nothing more than a personal proclivity, peculiarity or mannerism", and that he was merely "satisfying a personal urge".

Five years later, MacKinnon published a more detailed version of her argument.[26] In that later version, she pointed out that:

> As a practice, sexual harassment singles out a gender-defined group, women, for special treatment in a way which adversely affects and burdens their status as employees. Sexual harassment limits women in a way men are not limited. It deprives them of opportunities that are available to male employees without sexual conditions. In so doing, it creates two employment standards: one for women that includes sexual requirements, one for men that does not. From preliminary indications, large numbers of working women, regardless of characteristics which distinguish them from each other, report being sexually harassed. Most sexually harassed people are women. These facts indicate that the incidents are something more than "personal" and "unique" and have some connection to the female condition as a whole.[27]

In 1976, the year after MacKinnon circulated her first draft, the District of Columbia District Court offered encouragement to lobbyists, holding, in *Williams v. Saxbe*,[28] that sexual harassment clearly was "treatment based on sex" within the meaning of Title VII. That quite dramatic development was consolidated the following year when three federal Courts of Appeal handed down similar decisions.[29] In the *Barnes* case appeal,[30] for example, the Court held that not only was sexual harassment actionable under Title VII but also that employers could be held liable for the acts of their supervisory staff. Employers could, however, escape liability, the Court held, if the supervisory staff in question had contravened the employer's policy without his or her knowledge and the consequences were subsequently addressed and remedied

---

[26] Catharine A. MacKinnon, *Sexual Harassment of Working Women: A Case of Sex Discrimination*, (New Haven and London: Yale University Press, 1979).

[27] MacKinnon, *ibid.*, at 193.

[28] 413 F. Supp. 654 (D.C.C. 1976).

[29] *Barnes v. Costle*, 561 F. 2d 983 (D.C. Cir. 1977); *Garber v. Saxon Business Products*, 552 F. 2d 1032 (4th Cir. 1977); and *Tompkins v. Public Service Electric and Gas Co. (Tomkins II)*, 568 F. 2d 1044 (3rd Cir. 1977).

[30] *Barnes v. Costle, op. cit.*

when discovered. The reasoning of the Court in *Barnes* was almost identical to that of MacKinnon in her first draft. Holding for the complainant, the Court pointed out that:

> But for her womanhood, her participation in sexual activity would never have been solicited. To say, then, that she was victimized in her employment simply because she declined the invitation is to ignore the asserted fact that she was invited only because she was a woman subordinate to the inviter in the hierarchy of agency personnel. Put another way, she became the target of her superior's sexual desires because she was a woman and was asked to bow to his demands as the price for holding her job. The circumstance imparting high visibility to the role of gender in the affair is that no male employer was susceptible to such an approach by the appellant's supervisor.

By the mid-1980s, reasoning similar to MacKinnon's had been applied by courts or tribunals in Britain[31] and Northern Ireland[32] and her thesis is now almost universally accepted in common law jurisdictions. In this country the Labour Court based its groundbreaking decisions on sexual harassment on a MacKinnon-like interpretation of the Employment Equality Act, 1977. Section 3(1) of that Act provides that:

> A person who is an employer or who obtains under a contract with another person the services of employees of that other person shall not discriminate against an employee or a prospective employee or an employee of that other person in relation to access to employment, *conditions of employment* (other than remuneration or any condition relating to an occupational pension scheme), training or experience for or in relation to employment, promotion or re-grading in employment or classification of posts in employment.[33]

---

[31] See, for example, *Porcelli v. Strathclyde Regional Council*, [1984] I.R.L.R. 467.

[32] See, for example, *Mortiboys v. Crescent Garage Ltd.*, Industrial Tribunal, 34/83 SD (15 February, 1984). For a discussion of the decisions in *Porcelli, op. cit.*, and *Mortiboys, op. cit.*, see Deirdre Curtin, "Sexual Harassment in Employment, *loc. cit.*

[33] Emphasis added.

In a ground-breaking 1985 determination, the Labour Court stated in *A Worker v. A Garage Proprietor*[34] that:

> freedom from sexual harassment is a condition of work which an employee of either sex is entitled to expect. The court will, accordingly, treat any denial of that freedom as discrimination within the meaning of the Employment Equality Act, 1977.

The "Bisexual Defence"

Despite the fact that MacKinnon's once controversial theory is now accepted without question in most common law jurisdictions, it remains the case that express statutory prohibition of sexual harassment is preferable to strained interpretations of legislation such as the Irish Employment Equality Act, 1977, or the British Sex Discrimination Act, 1975. A curious anomaly concerning bisexual harassers serves to illustrate the somewhat limited and artificial nature of MacKinnon's sex discrimination thesis.

As has been pointed out above, sexual harassment is only outlawed under sex discrimination legislation where it can be characterised as activity leading to *discrimination* based on sex. If, however, an incident of harassment can be characterised as being based on sex but not as being discriminatory it arguably falls outside the scope of MacKinnon's thesis and, for that reason, outside the scope of the US Civil Rights Act, 1964, and the Employment Equality Act, 1977. It would seem that sexual harassment perpetrated by a bisexual harasser falls into this grey area, given that a bisexual who habitually harasses his or her fellow employees presumably does not discriminate between them on the basis of their sex. Such an individual's conduct, while sexually motivated, is not targeted at workers of a specific gender.

The "bisexual defence" theory was employed, with devastating effect, by Circuit Judge Bork in *Vinson v. Taylor*.[35] Holding that sexual harassment could never constitute a violation of Title VII, Judge Bork offered the following analysis of the law in support of his finding:

---

[34] EE 02/1985.

[35] 760 F. 2d 1330 (D.C. Cir., 1985).

Perhaps some of the doctrinal difficulty in this area is due to the awkwardness of classifying sexual advances as "discrimination." Harassment is reprehensible, but Title VII was passed to outlaw discriminatory behaviour and not simply behaviour of which we strongly disapprove. The artificiality of the approach we have taken appears from the decisions in this circuit. It is "discrimination" if a man makes unwanted sexual overtures to a woman, a woman to a man, a man to another man, or a woman to another woman. But this court has twice stated that Title VII does not prohibit sexual harassment by a "bisexual superior [because] the insistence upon sexual favours would ... apply to male and female employees alike." Thus, this court holds that only the differentiating libido runs afoul of Title VII, and bisexual harassment, however blatant and however offensive and disturbing, is legally permissible. Had Congress been aiming at sexual harassment, it seems unlikely that a woman would be protected from unwelcome heterosexual or lesbian advances but left unprotected when a bisexual attacks. That bizarre result suggests that Congress was not thinking of individual harassment at all but of discrimination in conditions of employment because of gender.[36]

Judge Bork's argument is both disturbingly convincing and compatible with the history of the development of sexual harassment law. If anything, his thesis becomes even more compelling when one considers MacKinnon's less than satisfactory response. Ignoring his consideration of the intention of Congress, MacKinnon simply addresses the issue of the "bisexual defence" as follows:

Originally it was argued that sexual harassment was not a proper gender claim because someone could harass both sexes. We argued that this was an issue of fact to be pleaded and proven, an issue of did he do this, rather than an issue of law, of whether he could have. The courts accepted that, creating this

---

[36] *Ibid.*, at 1333, n.7; Bork J., dissenting. Judges Scalia and Starr concurred with Judge Bork on the point in question. Bork discusses his somewhat controversial approaches to constitutional and statutory interpretation in his seminal work, *The Tempting of America: The Political Seduction of the Law* (New York: Touchstone, 1990).

kamikaze defence. To my knowledge, no one has used the bisexual defense since.[37]

MacKinnon's response may well have plugged the apparent hole in the dam wall for the time being. Problems such as the bisexual defence, however, continue to dog the development of any sexual harassment jurisprudence built on MacKinnon's foundations.[38] For a solid and unshakeable foundation upon which to build sexual harassment law, however, all interested parties, including MacKinnon, would argue that comprehensive legislation is required. It would seem that such legislation will soon be introduced in this jurisdiction.[39] The ambit of that legislation is, however, as yet unclear.

"QUID PRO QUO" HARASSMENT

All of the early successes in the American courts came in cases involving incidents of what has since become known as "quid pro quo" harassment. In essence, quid pro quo harassment "denotes an incidence in which sexual compliance is or is expected to be exchanged for a particular job opportunity. It forces an employee to choose between acceding to sexual demands or forfeiting job benefits, continued employment or promotion."[40] While quid pro quo harassment is not the only kind of sexual harassment now recognised by the courts it is certainly the most serious type. It was largely for that reason that quid pro quo harassment was the first kind of harassment to be judicially noted. For a number of

---

[37] Catharine A. MacKinnon, *Feminism Unmodified, op. cit.,* 108.

[38] For a discussion of other attacks on the "sexual harassment as sex discrimination" thesis see MacKinnon, *Feminism Unmodified, op. cit.,* at 103-116.

[39] In his speech at the launch of the Employment Equality Agency's 1994 Annual Report, the Minister for Equality and Law Reform, Mervyn Taylor, TD, stated that: "As part of the review of the Employment Equality Act of 1977 I intend to introduce more explicit provisions in relation to sexual harassment in order to strengthen the position for all employees who find themselves under stress as a result of this kind of unacceptable behaviour." Government Press Centre, Government Buildings, 26 June 1995.

[40] Deirdre Curtin, "Sexual Harassment in Employment", *op. cit.,* at 76.

years it remained the only kind of harassment which was recognised as sex discrimination within the meaning of Title VII. For
that reason, claimants in the late 1970s and early 1980s could
only win their cases if they could prove that they had suffered
tangible employment-related losses as a result of their rebuffing
the sexual advances of their supervisors. Despite this somewhat
limited definition of sexual harassment, substantial progress was
made in those early years. The *Tompkins* case,[41] for example,
involved a classical incident of quid pro quo harassment and, for
that reason, the decision of the court of first instance was overturned on appeal. In rejecting the decision of the District Court,
the Third Circuit held that:

> Title VII is violated when a supervisor with the actual or con-
> structive knowledge of the employer makes sexual advances or
> demands towards a subordinate employee and conditions that
> employee's job status — evaluation, continued employment,
> promotion, or other aspects of career development — on a fa-
> vourable response to those advances or demands, and the em-
> ployer does not take prompt and appropriate remedial action af-
> ter acquiring such knowledge.[42]

Given the nature of quid pro quo harassment it is not surprising
that many commentators have characterised sexual harassment
as an abuse of power, having more to do with power than sex. The
Employment Equality Agency, for example, subscribes to this
theory,[44] arguing in the recently launched *Code of Practice* on

---

[41] *Op. cit.*

[42] 568 F. 2d 1044 (3rd Cir. 1977).

[43] In the wake of the Anita Hill/Clarence Thomas case in America, for example, the *New York Times* argued that sexual harassment "has less to do
with sex than with power. It is a way to keep women in their place; through
harassment men devalue a woman's role in the work place by calling attention to her sexuality." Daniel Goleman, "Sexual Harassment: About Power,
Not Lust", *New York Times*, 22 October 1991; as cited in Mark A. Rothstein
and Lance Leibman, *Employment Law - Cases and Materials*, 3rd. ed., (New
York: Foundation Press, 1994), at 563. See generally, Nancy S. Ehrenreich,
"Pluralist Myths and Powerless Men: The Ideology of Reasonableness in
Sexual Harassment Law", (1990) 99 *Yale L.J.* 1177.

[44] *Cf.* Chapter 1.

sexual harassment that "[s]exual harassment is often misrepresented as sexually motivated behaviour; experience shows, however, that it results primarily from abuse of power."[46] Similar arguments have been advanced by the European Commission and, indeed, by the current Minister for Equality and Law Reform. While the "abuse of power" argument may be an attractive one, it is submitted that it lacks a solid factual foundation.[47] Sexual harassment is not only perpetrated by men in positions of power, but also by co-workers, inferiors and clients. In such circumstances, the harassment clearly has little to do with power and much to do with sex. As such cases continue to abound,[48] the "abuse of power" theory must be regarded as a potentially dangerous red herring which simply clouds more important issues. As MacKinnon observes:

> In workplaces, sexual harassment by supervisors of subordinates is common; in education, by administrators of lower-level administrators, by faculty of students. But it also happens among co-workers, from third parties, even by subordinates in the workplace, men who are women's hierarchical inferiors or peers. Basically, it is done by men to women regardless of relative position on the formal hierarchy.[49]

---

[45] Department of Equality and Law Reform, *Code of Practice: Measures to Protect the Dignity of Women and Men at Work*, (Dublin, 1994). While the *Code of Practice* was published by the Department of Equality and Law Reform it was drafted by the Employment Equality Agency.

[46] *Code of Practice, op. cit.*, at 9.

[47] *Cf.* Chapter 1.

[48] Dr. Louise FitzGerald, a psychologist at the University of Illinois, has suggested that "in less than five per cent of cases the harassment involves a bribe or threat for sex, where the man is saying, 'If you do this for me, I'll help you at work, and if you don't, I'll make things difficult for you.'" As quoted in Rothstein and Leibman, *Employment Law - Cases and Materials, op. cit.*, at 563.

[49] MacKinnon, *Feminism Unmodified, op. cit.*, 107.

"HOSTILE OR ABUSIVE ENVIRONMENT" HARASSMENT

The second type of sexual harassment which was recognised by the courts is referred to by commentators and lawyers as "condition of work" or "hostile or abusive environment" harassment, and involves "the persistent subjection of female employees to an intimidating, hostile or offensive working environment".[50] An abusive environment claim does not revolve around the denial of a specific employment benefit. It is characterised rather by multiple, although perhaps individually non-actionable, incidents of offensive conduct.[51]

Brown v. City of Guthrie[52] was the first American case in which abusive environment harassment was recognised as the major basis for the cause of action. Although Ms. Brown could not show a direct employment nexus, she was able to establish that the sexually harassing acts of her supervisor (such as the making of lewd comments, innuendos and gestures) substantially affected her emotional and psychological stability. This harassment, she argued, contributed to a work environment which was so unbearable that she was forced to resign.

The importance of the concept of abusive environment harassment was subsequently explained by the Court of Appeals for the District of Columbia in *Bundy v. Jackson*.[53] In that case the Court held that unless liability could attach for such harassment

> an employer could sexually harass a female employee with impunity by carefully stopping short of firing the employee or taking other tangible actions against her in response to her resistance, thereby creating the impression . . . that the employer did not take the ritual of harassment and resistance "seriously". . . .
> The law may allow a woman to prove that her resistance to the harassment cost her her job or some economic benefit, but this

---

[50] Footnote omitted.

[51] Deirdre Curtin, "Sexual Harassment in Employment", *loc. cit.*, at 76.

[52] 30 E.P.D. para. 33,031; 22 FEP 1631 (W.D. Okla., 1980).

[53] 641 F. 2d 934 (D.C. Cir. 1981).

will do her no good if the employer never takes such tangible actions against her."[54]

SEXUAL HARASSMENT AND THE US SUPREME COURT

In 1986 the US Supreme Court heard its first sexual harassment case: *Meritor Savings Bank v. Vinson.*[55] The plaintiff in *Meritor*[56] claimed that her supervisor had, *inter alia,* fondled her, followed her into the women's toilets, exposed himself to her and raped her on a number of occasions. This conduct, she stated, had ceased almost a year before she filed her suit. The employer denied that any of the events alleged by the plaintiff had ever taken place.

Given the decisions which had been handed down up to that point, the Bank would appear to have been on relatively solid ground in arguing that, even if her testimony was true, its employee could not succeed in an action under Title VII given that she had not suffered "economic" or "tangible" injury, despite the fact that the Supreme Court, as the highest court in the United States, is not bound by decisions handed down by inferior courts. In any event, the Court decided that employers could be found vicariously liable for acts of sexual harassment perpetrated by their supervisory employees, regardless of whether or not that harassment had resulted in "economic" or "tangible" injury being caused to the victim. The Court went on to point out that the crucial question which must be answered by any court in handing down its decision in such a case was "whether [the victim] by her conduct indicated that the alleged sexual advances were unwelcome, not whether her actual participation in sexual intercourse was voluntary."[57]

---

[54] *Op. cit.,* at 945.

[55] 106 S. Ct. 2399 (1986). For a discussion of the case see R.K. Robinson, K. Delaney and E.C. Stephens, "Hostile Environment: A Review of the Implications of *Meritor Savings Bank v. Vinson*", (1987) 38 *Labour Law Journal* 179.

[56] Interestingly, Ms. Vinson was represented by Catharine MacKinnon, among others.

[57] 106 S. Ct. 2399 at 2406.

In deciding *Meritor*,[58] the Supreme Court expressly approved of the principles laid down by the US Equal Employment Opportunities Commission in its "Guidelines on Sexual Harassment" of 1980.[59] Those guidelines, which have since been relied upon by the courts on numerous occasions,[60] provide that unlawful sexual harassment occurs when:

> a) submission to the conduct is either an explicit or implied term or condition of employment;
>
> b) submission to or rejection of such conduct by an individual is used as the basis for employment decisions affecting such individual; or
>
> c) such conduct has the purpose or effect of unreasonably interfering with an individual's work performance or creating an intimidating, hostile, or offensive working environment.[61]

While the Guidelines do not have the force of legislation and, for that reason, do not bind the courts, they were described in *Meritor* as being both "fully consistent with the existing case law"[62] and "a body of experience and informed judgement to which Courts and litigants may properly resort for guidance".[63] In expressly accepting the third leg of the EEOC's definition of sexual harassment the Court ensured that abusive environment harassment was recognised in law as constituting unlawful sex discrimination.

---

[58] *Op. cit.*

[59] E.E.O.C., Guidelines on Sexual Harassment as an amendment to the Guidelines on Discrimination Because of Sex, 29 C.F.R. 1604.11, 45 F.R. 25024 (1980).

[60] See, *inter alia, Bundy v. Jackson*, 641 F. 2d 934 (D.C. Cir. 1981); *Henson v. City of Dundee*, 682 F. 2d 897, (11th Cir. 1982); *Brown v. City of Guthrie*, 22 FEP 1631 (W.D. Okla. 1980).

[61] As cited in Aggarwal, *op. cit.,* at 26.

[62] *Op. cit.*, at 2405.

[63] *Ibid.*

The "Reasonable Woman" Test

In 1993, the case of *Harris v. Forklift Systems Inc.*[64] offered the Supreme Court a chance to reassess and expand upon its holding in *Meritor*. While the Court did not take the available opportunity to clearly map out previously uncharted areas of sexual harassment law, it did settle one particularly controversial issue. For some years employers had argued that it was both unrealistic and unfair to impose liability where women, who they viewed as being particularly sensitive, had found offensive or abusive, treatment which was regarded by most other women as falling short of constituting sexual harassment. On the other hand, there were lobbyists who argued that the courts should base their decisions on the actual impact of the conduct in question on the women who were on the receiving end of it. Employers regarded this latter argument as being somewhat illogical, pointing out that two women could be subjected to the same treatment and have different reactions with one having no complaint about the treatment and the other finding it offensive and abusive.[65] Only in the latter case would liability attach to the employer. Such differing treatment by the law of identical actions would, employers argued, make it impossible for them to define sexual harassment in workplace codes of conduct without prohibiting activities which the vast majority of workers of both genders enjoyed.

The Supreme Court's response was to hold that actionable sexual conduct under Title VII included that which a *reasonable* person would find hostile or abusive.[66] Not only must a reasonable person find the conduct hostile or abusive, however, but the

---

[64] 114 S. Ct. 367 (1993).

[65] As one English journalist has noted, "one woman's sexual harassment is another woman's unremarkable office banter." Zoe Heller, "Let's banish the boring solemnity of the sex-pest debate", *The Independent on Sunday,* 20 October 1991.

[66] (1993) 114 S. Ct. 367, at 370. For discussions of the "reasonable woman" test, see generally, Naomi R. Cahn, "The Looseness of Legal Language: The Reasonable Woman Standard in Theory and Practice", (1992) 77 *Cornell L. Rev.* 1398; and Nancy S. Ehrenreich, "Pluralist Myths and Powerless Men: The Ideology of Reasonableness in Sexual Harassment Law", (1990) 99 *Yale Law Journal* 1177.

individual plaintiff must have done so as well.[67] Unfortunately,
the Court offered little guidance as to when a "reasonable person"
will find conduct to be hostile or abusive. The difficulty which
arises as a result of the Court's reluctance to offer such guidance
is, as Reilly points out, that:

> [i]ndividual tastes regarding sexual conduct vary widely and
> conclusions about what a "reasonable person" or even a
> "reasonable woman" would find offensive or harmless in a given
> situation are precarious.[68]

Some clarification can be gleaned from earlier decisions of American federal courts. In *Rabidue v. Osceola Refining Company*,[69] for
example, the US Sixth Circuit held the trier of facts "must adopt
the perspective of a reasonable person's reaction to a similar environment under essentially like or similar circumstances." In *Yates
v. Avco Corp.*,[70] the same Court held that:

> in a sexual harassment case involving a male supervisor's har-
> assment of a female subordinate, it seems only reasonable that
> the person standing in the shoes of the employee should be the
> reasonable woman since the plaintiff in this type of case is re-
> quired to be a member of a protected class and is by definition
> female.[71]

In essence then, the American courts will uphold a claim of abusive environment harassment if it can be proved that the woman
who was subjected to the treatment complained of, found it to be
hostile or abusive conduct, and a reasonable woman in like or
similar circumstances would have found a similar environment to
be hostile or abusive.

Such a test would, in all the circumstances, appear to strike
the optimum balance between the positions of the radical wings of
employer and feminist lobby groups. It certainly has the advan-

---

[67] *Ibid.*, at 371.

[68] Reilly, *loc. cit.*

[69] 805 F. 2d 61; 41 E.P.D. para. 36,643 (6th Cir., 1986).

[70] 819 F. 2d 630; 43 E.P.D. para. 37,086 (6th Cir., 1987).

[71] At 637.

tage of ensuring that employers are not punished for acts committed by their employees which are, in the eyes of the vast majority of workers (both male *and* female), merely part and parcel of normal, non-abusive working environments. Unfortunately, however, the American test has not been adopted on this side of the Atlantic.

In England, as Bourne and Whitmore point out:

> [t]he standard of behaviour which might constitute . . . sexual harassment is . . . to be viewed from the point of view of the victim. . . . Standards will vary as to what constitutes sexual harassment.[72]

Bourne and Whitmore's assessment of the of the legal position in England is quite consistent with the caselaw in that jurisdiction. In *Wileman v. Milinec Engineering Ltd.,*[73] for example, Popplewell J. considered the issue of different women reacting differently to identical treatment and held that if the alleged harasser

> made sexual remarks to a number of people, it has to be looked at in the context of each person. All the people to whom they are made may regard them as wholly inoffensive; everyone else may regard them as offensive. Each individual then has the right, if the remarks are regarded as offensive, to treat them as an offence under the Sex Discrimination Act 1975.[74]

Mr. Justice Popplewell's decision contrasts sharply with the earlier decision of Lord Justice May in *De Souza v. Automobile Association,*[75] a racial harassment case. In *De Souza* it was held that, for a case to succeed:

---

[72] Colin Bourne & John Whitmore, *Race and Sex Discrimination*, 2nd ed., (London: Sweet and Maxwell, 1993), at 140.

[73] [1988] I.R.L.R. 145.

[74] *Ibid.*, at 147. In *Wileman* the Employment Appeals Tribunal also held that a court or tribunal could also take into account the fact that the complainant often wore scanty and "provocative" clothing at work in assessing whether the harassment to which she was subjected constituted a detriment. A tribunal, it held, is entitled to look at the circumstances in which remarks are made which are said to constitute a detriment.

[75] [1986] I.R.L.R. 103.

the court or [t]ribunal must find that by reason of the act or acts complained of a reasonable worker would or might take the view that he had thereby been disadvantaged in the circumstances in which he had thereafter to work.[76]

Quite unusually, then, it would seem that English courts and tribunals apply quite different tests in sexual and racial harassment cases. It is submitted that the approach they take to racial harassment cases, which more closely reflects the American test, is the better one. At the very least, it has that element of objectivity which characterises the most enduring and widely accepted legal tests.

For all its inherent problems, the Irish Labour Court would seem to prefer the subjective test so beloved of Mr. Justice Popplewell. In *A Company v. A Worker*,[77] a 1992 determination, the Court stated that:

> Irrespective of the attitude of other workers to such matters, each employee has the right to work in an environment free from sexual harassment and therefore has the individual right to determine whether and from whom, if anybody, she will accept such conduct. To exercise this right, however, the worker must make known to the offender that his conduct is unwanted.

Until the matter is addressed either by the Supreme Court or the legislature the conflict between the subjective and "reasonable woman" tests will not be finally resolved. In the meantime, the wisest course of action for employers is to presume that the Labour Court will continue to lean towards the subjective test.

PORNOGRAPHY

The display of pornographic materials in the workplace, such as the hanging of calendars or posters depicting nude or semi-nude women, has long been a controversial matter. In *Rabidue v. Osceola Refining Company*,[78] for example, the US Sixth Circuit

---

[76] *Ibid.*, at 107.

[77] *A Company v. A Worker*, EEO492, 9 March 1992.

[78] 805 F. 2d 611 (6th Cir., 1986).

refused to hold that the presence of pornographic images in a workplace resulted in the creation of an abusive environment. In so deciding, the Court acknowledged that "it cannot seriously be disputed that in some work environments, humour and language are rough hewn and vulgar. Sexual jokes, sexual conversations, and girlie magazines may abound."[79] The Court went on, however, to hold that "Title VII was not meant to, nor can, change this."[80]

It now seems beyond doubt, however, that courts in most jurisdictions will regard the display of such materials as poisoning the working environment and enhancing the case of any employee bringing proceedings against her employer for abusive environment harassment. The reason for the adoption of such a stance by courts and tribunals seems clear. As has been argued elsewhere:

> Stories of women in nontraditional fields such as the trades demonstrate that pornography is often used by men in the workplace to send messages to the women that they do not belong there.[81] The existence of pornography in the workplace may undermine a woman's sense of self-worth and make the conditions of her employment either unbearable or devastating for her self-esteem.[82] It may drive women out of male-dominated workplaces that are badly in need of integration.[83]

In America, several lower federal courts have now concluded that evidence of pornography in the workplace may serve to support claims of abusive environment harassment under Title VII.[84] In 1988, for example, the Court of Appeals held, in *Bennett v. Corron*

---

[79] 41 E.P.D. para 36,643 (6th Cir., 1986).

[80] *Ibid.*

[81] Footnote omitted.

[82] Footnote omitted.

[83] Note, "Pornography, Equality, and a Discrimination-Free Workplace: A Comparative Perspective", (1993) 106 *Harvard Law Review* 1075, at 1086-87.

[84] See *Andrews v. City of Philadelphia*, 895 F. 2d 1469, 1485 (3rd Cir., 1990); *Waltman v. International Paper Co.*, 875 F. 2d 468, 477 & n.3 (5th Cir., 1989). But, see also *Rabidue v. Osceola Ref. Co.*, 805 F. 2d 611, 622 (6th Cir., 1986) (dismissing the effect of pornography on the workplace as "de minimis"), cert. denied, 481 US 1041 (1987).

& *Black Corp.*,[85] that graffiti, in the form of cartoons depicting men and women in sexually demeaning postures, created a hostile working environment.[86] The Court specifically stated that

> any reasonable person would have to regard these cartoons as highly offensive to a woman who seeks to deal with her fellow employees and clients with professional dignity and without the barrier of sexual differentiation and abuse.[87]

The Irish Labour Court has taken a similar approach to the matter, holding in *A Company v. A Worker*,[88] that

> the display of an explicit calendar [as well as other conduct] . . . had sexual connotations and, if offensive to the worker concerned, constituted sexual harassment.

The most detailed judgement to have been delivered on the pornography issue to date would, however, appear to be that handed down in the American case of *Robinson v. Jacksonville Shipyards Inc.*[89] Lois Robinson was a female welder and one of only a handful of women who held skilled crafts positions at the shipyards.[90] Robinson worked in an environment which was described as being immersed in pornography. Photographs of nude women in submissive poses covered the walls and salesmen who did business with the shipyards regularly distributed their firms' promotional "pin-up" calendars to employees, who were encouraged by the company to hang them up at work. Many of the photographs depicted explicit and violent scenes which were demeaning to women. None of them depicted men.

---

[85] 845 F. 2d 105 (1988).

[86] See also *Waltman v. International Paper Co.*, 875 F. 2d 468; 50 E.P.D. para. 39,106 (5th Cir., 1989), in which the US Fifth Circuit held that the presence of sexual graffiti in the plant constituted the existence of a hostile working environment.

[87] At 106.

[88] *A Company v. A Worker*, EEO492, 9 March 1992.

[89] 760 F. Supp. 1486 (M.D. Fla., 1991).

[90] The shipyard employed 2 women and 958 men as skilled craftsworkers in 1980 and 6 women and 846 men in such positions in 1986.

Several of these photographs were placed by her co-workers in Robinson's working area, on the box where she left her tools, or handed to her directly in front of male colleagues in an attempt to humiliate her. One of Robinson's co-workers taunted her with a photograph of a nude woman with long blonde hair holding a whip. Because the plaintiff had long blonde hair and worked with a tool which was referred to as a "whip", she regarded the man's actions as constituting a personal threat. She complained to her employer on a number of occasions that she found the pornographic pictures both "degrading and humiliating". Her requests that the offending photographs be removed were ignored by management. Instead, her requests only prompted her male colleagues to bring in what was referred to in court as "hard pornography".

In the Federal District Court, Melton J. opined that the working environment in the shipyards amounted to a "visual assault on the sensibilities of female workers"[91] and went on to hold that any policy which allowed such materials to be displayed in the workplace contradicted the spirit of Title VII. In so finding he stated that:

> Pornography creates a barrier to the progress of women in the workplace because it conveys the message that they do not belong, that they are welcome in the workplace only if they subvert their identities to the sexual stereotypes prevalent in that environment. . . .[92] Pornography on an employer's wall or desk communicates a message about the way he views women, a view strikingly at odds with the way women wish to be viewed in the workplace. . . . It may communicate that women should be the objects of sexual aggression, that they are submissive slaves to male desires, or that their most salient and desirable attributes are sexual. . . . All of the views to some extent detract from the image most women in the workplace would like to project: that of the professional, credible co-worker.[93]

---

[91] *Op. cit.*, at 1495.

[92] At 1523.

[93] At 1527.

Judge Melton determined that such an atmosphere was "no less destructive to and offensive to workplace equality than a sign declaring 'Men Only.'"[94] Judge Melton ordered the company to implement a sexual harassment prevention policy that mandated removing of all materials which were "sexually suggestive, sexually demeaning, or pornographic."[95]

While the legal position in relation to the display of pornographic materials in the workplace is not definitively settled, and the Irish Labour Court has certainly not defined what it sees as constituting pornography, it seems unlikely that the direction in which common law courts have been consistently heading in the last few years will change. While the issue is still the subject of public debate, such is only the case because of a combination of ignorance, misinformation and sensationalist reporting in newspapers. In 1994, following the publication of the Department of Equality and Law Reform's *Code of Practice* on sexual harassment,[96] a number of newspapers published articles condemning what they regarded as a campaign to ban harmless "girlie magazines".

Typical of the kind of sensationalist reporting in some newspapers was an article by Declan Lynch published in the *Sunday Independent*, which stated that:

> [i]t will be a wretched day indeed when we are reduced to calling the guards when we go into our local garage and see a wall plastered with pictures of naked people in compromising positions.[97]

It is hard to fathom how Mr. Lynch managed to determine from reading the Code that the Department of Equality and Law Reform, the Employment Equality Agency, ICTU, IBEC or any other interested party was suggesting that the display of pornographic materials in the workplace should be deemed to be a criminal of-

---

[94] *Ibid.*

[95] At 1542.

[96] *Op. cit.*

[97] Declan Lynch, "No nudes is bad news", *The Sunday Independent*, 26 September 1994

fence which would require that the Gardaí be called in to work-places. More subtle, however, was the use of the words "naked people" rather than "naked women", given that the overwhelming majority of pornographic materials to be found in garages and other workplaces in this country depict women.

While newspaper articles, such as Mr. Lynch's, may raise the issue of sexual harassment in the public domain and thereby prompt consideration of the issues involved, it is certainly argu-able that the kind of approach many of them take to the matter is both misleading and damaging to efforts made by organisations such as the Employment Equality Agency to promote anti-discrimination policies.

THE INTENTION OF THE HARASSER

In the course of the kind of public debate on sexual harassment mentioned above, men often argue that they are surprised at some of the types of conduct which women regard as constituting sexual harassment. On foot of that complaint, it is sometimes ar-gued that courts and tribunals should, in the absence of a "reasonable woman" test in this jurisdiction, take the intention of the man in pursuing his course of conduct into account. The sug-gestion would appear to be that complainants should have to prove that the perpetrators of the acts in question intended to harass them. That argument certainly has parallels in other ar-eas of the law. In criminal trials, for example, the prosecutor is required to prove that the defendant had what is known as the necessary *mens rea,* or intention,[98] to commit the crime with which he or she is charged. Sexual harassment suits under the Irish Employment Equality Act, 1977, the English Sex Discrimi-nation Act, 1975, and Title VII of the American Civil Rights Act, however, are civil suits rather than criminal prosecutions. In civil suits proof of *mens rea* is not required. Rather, depending on the type of case which is involved, the plaintiff simply needs to prove that the defendant was negligent, reckless or simply responsible. In such a context, the arguments of those who advocate the im-position of a duty on complainants to prove that the harasser had

---

[98] Literally translated "mens rea" means something closer to "state of mind".

a particular *mens rea* become less persuasive. In any case, such arguments have simply not been accepted by the courts in Britain[99] and America, while it would, on balance, appear that they are unlikely to be accepted by the Irish High and Supreme Courts.

In *Strathclyde Regional Council v. Porcelli*,[100] for example, Lord Justice Emslie held that the Sex Discrimination Act, 1975, is simply concerned with the "treatment" to which the victim is subjected and not with the motive or objective of the person responsible for that treatment. There need not, he held, be a sex related purpose in the mind of a person who indulges in unwanted and objectionable sexual overtures to a woman or exposes her to offensive sexual jokes. Rather, it is enough if the treatment occurs because she is a woman. Describing such treatment as a "sexual sword", Lord Justice Grieve held that "it was clear that the wound it inflicted [on Ms. Porcelli] was more than a mere scratch, the conclusion must be that the sword had been unsheathed and used because the victim was a woman."[101]

HARASSMENT OF MEN

As Marie Reilly of the University of South Carolina points out, "[s]exual harassment, however defined, is an unusual social problem in that one group of people engage in the challenged conduct and another group bears the loss, with virtually no overlap.

---

[99] For that reason, Hewson concludes that "it is no defence that the harasser did not intend to harass the complainant." Barbara Hewson, "A recent problem ?" (1995) *New Law Journal* 626.

[100] [1986] I.R.L.R. 365.

[101] *Ibid.*, at 139. The decision in *Porcelli* was expressly approved of by Margaret Monaghan, Equality Officer, in *A Limited Company v. One Female Employee* (the "Killarney" case), EE10/1988, 30 December 1988. The Labour Court has, however, confused the matter somewhat, holding, in *A Company v. A Worker*, EEO492, 9 March 1992, that "For it to be established that the conduct complained of was discrimination by what amounted to sexual harassment, the worker must establish either directly or on the balance of probabilities that the alleged conduct took place, that it was offensive to and unwanted by her, and that the alleged perpetrators knew or could reasonably have been expected to know that it was offensive and unwanted."

The groups are easily identified as men and women."[102] Reilly is quite correct in concluding that the overwhelming majority of the victims of sexual harassment are women.[103] That is not, however, to say that there have not been a number of successful sexual harassment suits brought by men against their employers as a result of acts perpetrated by women employees. In *Nelson v. Reisher*,[104] for example, the US Fourth Circuit held that a female supervisor and co-workers had created a "hostile environment" for the male victim because of their numerous criticisms and reprimands of him over a three-year period, while the Irish Labour Court awarded a male complainant £1,000 in 1992 after finding that a female Company Director had sexually harassed him in threatening to send him on errands for condoms and asking him to complete a "sex survey."[105]

While the incidence of men bringing sexual harassment suits against their employers remains extremely low in comparison to the number of suits instigated by women, employers should note that, at least to date, the Labour Court has not drawn any distinctions between the two types of cases. It is highly unlikely that they will alter their stance on the matter at any stage in the future.

SAME-SEX HARASSMENT

If the incidence of sexual harassment of men by women is relatively low, the percentage of reported cases involving same-sex harassment (that is harassment of men by men or of women by women) can only be referred to as infinitesimal. While Meenan states that "the matter of harassment between members of the

---

[102] Reilly, *loc. cit.*, at 428.

[103] See Preface.

[104] (4th Cir. 1989), 88-1133.

[105] *A Company v. A Worker*, EEO992, 22 July, 1992. See Martin Frawley, "Compensation for Male Apprentice in Sexual Harassment Case", (1992) 42 *Industrial Relations News*.

same sex is unclear,"[106] the Labour Court would seem to have indicated its opinion on the matter. In *A Worker v. A Company*[107]
the Court observed that:

> [I]nherent in any case of sexual harassment is a perceived domi-
> nant position of a person of one sex over a person of the opposite
> sex, whether that dominance be attributed to the historical roles
> of males and females or to a position of authority in the work-
> place. The court also considers that the detrimental effect of sex-
> ual harassment on the victim, whatever its measure, derives ba-
> sically from the fact that the offender is of the opposite sex, and
> that inherent in the harassment is innuendo or threat to the vic-
> tim of a sexual nature. In this case, while the offensive remarks
> made by the general manager were demeaning to the worker as
> a woman they do not come within the scope of the accepted
> meaning of sexual harassment — the unwanted real, implied, or
> perceived request for, or threat of extracting, sexual favours.
> Where two persons of the same sex are involved, it is the court's
> view that particular circumstances must be established to justify
> the claim that the conduct of one constitutes sexual harassment
> of the other.[108]

Unfortunately, the Court failed to elaborate on its determination
and spell out exactly what those "particular circumstances" might
be. The determination in *A Worker v. A Company* would certainly
seem to be far from satisfactory, in that its assertion that "the
detrimental effect of sexual harassment on the victim . . . derives
. . . from the fact that the offender is of the opposite sex" seems
quite absurd. It was certainly not backed up by empirical or other
evidence and must be viewed as being open to challenge in future
same-sex harassment cases.

Despite the Labour Court's holding it is submitted that any
logical future decision of the High or Supreme Courts to be delivered on the matter will, almost certainly, go the other way. As has
already been pointed out, the Employment Equality Act, 1977,

---

[106] Frances Meenan, *Working Within the Law,* (Dublin: Oak Tree Press,
1994), 129.

[107] (1992) 3 Employment Law Reports 40; EEO 3/1991.

[108] *Ibid.*, at 44.

prohibits discrimination based on the gender of the employee. That prohibition is certainly not limited by reference to the sexual orientation of the individual who acts in a discriminatory manner. Implied acceptance of such an approach is evident from the decisions of courts and tribunals in both Britain and the United States. In Britain, for example, the first successful same-sex harassment suit concluded in 1993 when a security guard was awarded £4,500 in damages after his male supervisor "grabbed him from behind and simulated intercourse",[109] while even Judge Bork in America was willing to accept that if MacKinnon's thesis held water in relation to heterosexual harassment, then it also did so in relation to homosexual harassment.[110]

Until the matter has been clarified, either in legislation or by one of the superior courts, it is probably safer for victims of same-sex harassment to steer clear of the Labour Court and pursue their claims in the Employment Appeals Tribunal under the Unfair Dismissals Acts, 1977-1993, rather than under the Employment Equality Act. In such cases the claimant argues that her employer's conduct, or the conduct of a co-worker which was condoned or permitted by her employer, amounted to constructive dismissal, and was unfair within the meaning of the 1977 and 1993 Acts.

HARASSMENT BY INDIVIDUALS OTHER THAN CO-WORKERS

As Meenan points out, the

> . . . Labour Court has taken a wide view of sexual harassment, [accepting that] it [need] not necessarily [be] caused directly by the employer or an employee within the company. In fact, it can happen where a person enters the [workplace] at the invitation of the employer and harasses an employee.[111]

Meenan's assessment of the Labour Court's position accurately reflects its determination in a 1991 case, *A Worker v. A Com-*

---

[109] *Gates v. Security Express*, Industrial Tribunal, 21 June 1993.

[110] *Vinson v. Taylor, op. cit.*

[111] Meenan, *op. cit.*, 130

pany.[112] The complainant in that case was employed by the defendant company as a book-keeper and office worker from June, 1981, until March, 1991. She testified before the court that she had, over a period of two to three years leading up to March, 1990, been physically sexually assaulted and subjected to harassment of a sexual nature by Mr. B., "a person to whom the general manager of the company had granted permission to use the company's premises and facilities for his own business purposes."[113] The plaintiff had complained to the company's female general manager about Mr. B.'s conduct on a number of occasions. The plaintiff's complaints had no effect, however, and it wasn't until "the entire female staff of the company took industrial action in protest that the general manager barred Mr. B. from the company's premises."

The Labour Court was satisfied that Mr. B.'s conduct constituted "sexual harassment of a most abusive kind."[114] On the crucial issue of whether or not the company was liable for the actions of Mr. B. the Court determined that it was

> irrelevant that the perpetrator of the harassment was not an employee of the company. He was on the company premises with the agreement of the employer and the employer was in a position to protect the worker. . . . In failing to protect the worker against the harassment prior to the industrial action, the employer had in effect imposed discriminatory conditions of employment on the worker.[115]

While the Labour Court's approach to determining third party sexual harassment cases is both admirable and consistent with the decisions of courts in other jurisdictions, the relatively recent decision of Mr. Justice Costello of the High Court in *The Health Board v. BC and the Labour Court*,[116] would seem to have altered most lawyers understanding of the legal position in relation to

---

[112] (1992) 3 Employment Law Reports 40; EEO 3/1991.

[113] At 42.

[114] At 43.

[115] *Ibid.*

[116] Unreported, Costello J., High Court, 19 January 1994.

such incidents. Mr. Justice Costello's decision is discussed in considerable detail in Chapter Three. For the moment, it is sufficient to note that third party sexual harassment suits are unlikely to be successful in Ireland, at least in the immediate future.

Figure 2.1 includes some of the key findings on sexual harassment and the law in Ireland.

Figure 2.1: Sexual Harassment and the Law in Ireland

A person who is an employer or who obtains under a contract with another person the services of employees of that other person shall not discriminate against an employee or a prospective employee or an employee of that other person in relation to access to employment, conditions of employment (other than remuneration or any condition relating to an occupational pension scheme), training or experience for or in relation to employment, promotion or re-grading in employment or classification of posts in employment.
— Section 3(1), Employment Equality Act, 1977.

[F]reedom from sexual harassment is a condition of work which an employee of either sex is entitled to expect. The court will, accordingly, treat any denial of that freedom as discrimination within the meaning of the Employment Equality Act, 1977.
— Labour Court, *A Worker v. A Garage Proprietor*, EE 02/1985.

Irrespective of the attitude of other workers to such matters, each employee has the right to a work environment free from sexual harassment and therefore has the individual right to determine whether and from whom, if anybody, she will accept such conduct. To exercise this right, however, the worker must make known to the offender that his conduct is unwanted.
— Labour Court, *A Company v. A Worker*, EEO492, 9 March 1992.

[T]he display of an explicit calendar . . . had sexual connotations and, if offensive to the worker concerned, constituted sexual harassment
— Labour Court, *A Company v. A Worker*, EEO492, 9 March 1992

[I]nherent in any case of sexual harassment is a perceived dominant position of a person of one sex over a person of the opposite sex, whether that dominance be attributed to the historical roles of males and females or to a position of authority in the workplace. The court also considers that the detrimental effect of sexual harassment on the victim, whatever its measure, derives basically from the fact that the offender is of the opposite sex, and that inherent in the harassment is innuendo or threat to the victim of a sexual nature. In this case, while the offensive remarks made by the general manager were demeaning to the worker as a woman they do not come within the scope of the accepted meaning of sexual harassment — the unwanted real, implied, or perceived request for, or threat of extracting, sexual favours. Where two persons of the same sex are involved, it is the court's view that particular circumstances must be established to justify the claim that the conduct of one constitutes sexual harassment of the other.

— Labour Court, *A Worker v. A Company*, (1992) 3 Employment Law Reports 40, at 44.

CHAPTER THREE

EMPLOYERS' LIABILITY, DEFENCES AND REMEDIES

[T]he cost of precaution generally is much lower than the expected cost of the injury. . . . [I]mposing liability on the employer for the employee's acts without regard to the employer's fault makes economic sense.[1]

INTRODUCTION

The first question which any court or tribunal must ask itself in considering a sexual harassment case is whether or not the claimant was actually sexually harassed, within the meaning attributed to that term by the law. That is not, however, the only question which the court or tribunal must consider. The second, and equally important, question is whether or not the claimant's employer is legally liable for any harassment which occurred. It is as a result of the answer given by the courts to this second question that many otherwise sound claims have fallen. For that reason, it is extremely important that potential claimants or defendants not only assess whether or not an incident or incidents of sexual harassment have occurred, but also whether or not the employer in question is liable for that harassment.

Two further matters must also be considered. The first is that of the defences which can be raised by employers, while the second is that of the range of remedies which victims of sexual harassment can seek. Each of these issues is dealt with below.

---

[1] Marie T. Reilly, "A Paradigm for Sexual Harassment: Toward the Optimal Level of Loss" (1994) 47 *Vanderbilt Law Review* 427, at 453.

VICARIOUS LIABILITY[2]

Where the perpetrator of an act of sexual harassment is the employer himself then he is clearly legally liable for his actions. So, for example, if a shop owner sexually harasses an employee, he will be found liable for that harassment, provided that the victim can prove that, on the balance of probabilities, the harassment actually occurred. The situation is, however, somewhat different in respect of harassment perpetrated by an employee rather than by the employer himself. In such instances, the victim must prove that the employer is "vicariously liable." Holding an individual to be "vicariously liable" essentially means holding them liable for the acts of another party under their control. As McMahon and Binchy explain:

> The law is sometimes prepared to hold one person liable for the wrong committed by another person even though the person held liable is not at fault in the accepted sense of the word. Thus the law may hold the master liable for the wrongs of his servant, or the principal liable for the wrongs of his agent[] or the firm liable for the wrongs of its partner, in spite of the fact that the master, the principal or the firm may not have been at fault in any way . . . . [T]he concept of vicarious liability has dovetailed nicely with the more modern ideas that the person who creates the risk . . . should bear the loss. Such persons or enterprises are in a good position to absorb and distribute the loss by price controls and through proper liability insurance. Liability in these cases should, it is felt, follow "the deep pocket".[3]

While the Labour Court have, on a number of occasions, considered the issue of vicarious liability in the context of sexual harassment, the relevant principles have been most authoritatively mapped out by the High Court. In *The Health Board v. B.C. and the Labour Court*,[4] Mr. Justice Costello, as he then was, consid-

---

[2] See, generally, Laski, "The Basis of Vicarious Liability", (1916) 26 *Yale L.J.* 105; and Williams, "Vicarious Liability: Tort of the Master or the Servant?", (1956) 72 *Law Quarterly Review* 522.

[3] Bryan McMahon and William Binchy, *Irish Law of Torts*, 2nd ed., (Dublin: Butterworths, 1990), 748.

[4] Unreported, Costello J., High Court, 19 January 1994.

ered the ambit of an employer's liability for sexual harassment perpetrated by two of its employees. In so doing, he substantially redefined what had, prior to that case, been regarded by both the Labour Court and the Employment Equality Agency as the relevant legal principles.

The Health Board v. B.C.: **The Facts**

From the beginning of October, 1989, B.C., a female employee of the Health Board who had been in the Board's employment for fifteen years, was subjected to "lewd and coarse" remarks by two male colleagues. The men in question also, in the words of Mr. Justice Costello, "touched her without her consent and generally harassed her." While the claimant made no complaint to management she threatened the harassers that she would do so if they continued to act in such a manner. On 18 November 1989, the two men violently sexually assaulted her. It would appear from the judgement that the first man threw her onto a bed and held her down by the ankles while the second "held her shoulder down and then grossly indecently assaulted her."[5] The claimant immediately complained to management who conducted an investigation into the matter. The harassers admitted their guilt and, as a result, one was dismissed while the other was suspended without pay for five weeks. The matter was reported to the Gardaí who subsequently prosecuted the individuals responsible for the assault. Mr. Justice Costello concluded on the basis of the evidence before him that the "assault had a devastating effect on the claimant and she was out of work for nearly a year after it took place."

The Labour Court Determination

Given the Labour Court's previous track record in respect of sexual harassment cases, B.C. must, at the time, have appeared to have had a strong *prima facie* case against the Board under the Employment Equality Act, 1977. Following a finding in her favour by an Equality Officer,[6] however, the Board appealed the case to

---

[5] *Per* Costello J.

[6] See EE 22/1991.

the Labour Court and, ultimately, to the High Court on a point of law. The issue at the heart of both appeals was that of the employer's liability for the acts of its employees.

The Labour Court has, on a number of occasions, stated that employers have "a duty to ensure that employees enjoy working conditions free from sexual harassment." It has, for that reason, been quite willing to impose on employers liability for acts of sexual harassment perpetrated by their employees. In dealing with such cases, however, "it does and will take into account steps taken by employers to eliminate and prevent sexual harassment in the work place."[7] In the instant case the Court again briefly outlined its views on the matter:

> Whilst accepting that an employer cannot guarantee total prevention of harassment, the Court will look for and take note of what steps have been taken. The adoption of a Code of Practice, the adoption of a policy statement on the prevention of sexual harassment, the existence of guidelines as to how all staff should behave, and the establishment of clear grievance procedures, all constitute the kind of "reasonable steps" which employers should adopt and which will be accepted by the Court as evidence of the employer's *bona fides* in this type of dispute. Clearly, information about steps must be widely circulated in the place of work and information on the employer's attitude to acts of sexual harassment made available to all staff.[8]

Before the assault on B.C. had taken place the Health Board had issued guidelines to its supervisors on how to deal with "complaints of discrimination." The guidelines did not, however, indicate how supervisors should attempt to ensure that incidents of sexual harassment did not occur. Neither were employees informed of the procedures to be adopted if they found themselves to be victims of sexual harassment. For that reason, the Labour Court stated that it did not consider "that the action of the Board in instructing supervisors and top management as to how complaints of [sexual harassment] should be dealt with constituted 'reasonable steps'".

---

[7] *The Health Board v. B.C. and the Labour Court, op. cit.*

[8] *Ibid.*

In conclusion, the Court agreed

> with the findings of the Equality Officer that the claimant was mistreated by the two male employees; that this treatment was sexually offensive and was a form of harassment directly related to the claimant's sex and constituted less favourable treatment of her because of her sex.

The Court's decision, however, was to be overturned on appeal in the High Court.

The Decision of the High Court
In the High Court Mr. Justice Costello held that

> . . . the conduct of the Board's employees towards the claimant in this case prior to the 18 November 1989 (the date of the most serious assault) clearly constituted sexual harassment as the concept is ordinarily understood and clearly had a detrimental effect on the conditions in which she worked.

Somewhat surprisingly, however, he went on to opine (albeit *obiter dicta)* that

> [i]f an employee suddenly rapes a fellow employee it seems . . . that it would be a most imprecise use of language to describe him as having "harassed" her — his conduct would have amounted to an act different in kind to what is meant by that term.

In an interesting observation on the issue in question, Flynn comments that:

> The reluctance of Costello J. to describe rape as a form of sexual harassment is understandable and commendable in some respects. There would be the danger of diminishing the harrowing experience of a rape-survivor in these circumstances if the events were reduced to an incident of sexual harassment. Notwithstanding that legitimate anxiety, this portion of the judgement overlooks the fact, already referred to by the judge, that the term "sexual harassment" appears nowhere in the 1977 Act. Sexual harassment is one instance of sex discrimination and, although in the wake of s.4 of the Criminal Law (Rape)(Amendment) Act, 1990, a person of either sex can be found in law to have been raped, there is no doubt that women are overwhelmingly the victims of rape. Rape, in addition to infringing a woman's right to

bodily integrity, is also a violation of her right to equality, and that is a form of sex discrimination. Although rape and sexual assault do not fall within the four corners of the term "sexual harassment" as it is ordinarily employed in Ireland, this does not, in itself, exclude the possibility that the 1977 Act could be invoked. It is submitted that the observations of Costello J. in the case are incomplete in this respect.[9]

Veering away from the issue, however, Costello J. decided to "assume for the purpose of the case" that the assault on 18 November could be regarded as part of a course of conduct which could reasonably be regarded as "amounting to an act of sexual harassment."

In a dramatic, if not wholly unpredictable,[10] passage, Mr. Justice Costello went on to decline to hold the Health Board vicariously liable for the acts of its employees. While the judge accepted that the acts complained of amounted to acts of "discrimination" within the meaning of section 2 of the Employment Equality Act, 1977, he highlighted the fact that the legislation only prohibits such acts where they are committed by employers and that the Board "only infringed the section if it was vicariously liable for what its employees did. . . ." Whereas the Labour Court had gone on, at this point, to apply a test which Costello J. compared to that laid down in section 41 of the British Sex Discrimination Act, 1975,[11] he himself preferred to re-emphasise the importance of

---

[9] Leo Flynn, "The Limits of Sexual Harassment Liability", (1994) *Irish Law Times* 215.

[10] See further, Adrian F. Twomey, "Decision exposes gap in law on sexual harassment", *The Cork Examiner*, 28 January 1994. See also Adrian F. Twomey, "Work and the Law", in Noel Harvey, *Effective Supervisory Management in Ireland* (Dublin: NCIR Press, 1994), 243, at 253-254.

[11] Section 41 provides that "anything done by a person in the course of his employment shall be treated for the purposes of this Act as done by his employer as well as by him, whether or not it was done with the employer's knowledge or consent. . . . In proceedings brought under this Act in respect of an act alleged to have been done by an employee of his it shall be a defence for that person to prove that he took such steps as were reasonably practicable to prevent the employee from doing that act, or from doing in the course of his employment acts of that description."

the standard common law test applied in cases involving allegations of vicarious liability in this country:

> In the absence of express statutory provision the law in this
> country in relation to the liability of an employee for the tortious
> acts (including statutory torts) of his employee is perfectly clear -
> an employer is vicariously liable where the act is committed
> within the scope of his employment. . . . What the Labour Court
> should have done was to consider whether the employees were
> acting within the scope of their employment when they commit-
> ted the violent sexual assault on the claimant on the 18 Novem-
> ber. This question admits of only one answer. An employer may,
> of course, be vicariously liable when his employee is acting negli-
> gently, or even criminally. . . . But I cannot envisage any em-
> ployment in which they were engaged in respect of which a sex-
> ual assault could be regarded as so connected with it as to
> amount to an act within its scope. The Board is not therefore vi-
> cariously liable for what occurred.[12]

In seeking to justify his decision, Costello J. referred to a 1987
Department of Labour Discussion Document which stated that
"the question of whether a provision specifying the extent of an
employer's liability for the behaviour of an employee should be
included in the [1977] Act merits consideration". He further referred to Deirdre Curtin's observation that "one of the major la-
cunae in the . . . Act is the absence of an express provision rendering employers liable for the discriminatory acts of their employees".[13] Accordingly, Costello J. allowed the Health Board's appeal
and discharged the Labour Court's award of compensation to the
claimant.

Reaction to the Decision
The High Court decision attracted substantial media coverage
with front page stories being run by a number of newspapers.[14]

---

[12] *Per* Costello J. in *The Health Board v. B.C. and the Labour Court, op. cit.*

[13] Deirdre Curtin, *Irish Employment Equality Law*, (Dublin: Round Hall
Press, 1989), at 286.

[14] See, for example, "Sex pest decision court surprise", *The Irish Independent*,
20 January 1994, and "Sex harassment case causes concern", *The Evening*

Reaction from trade union representatives was not slow to follow either with Noirín Greene of SIPTU, for example, stating that

> [t]his decision clearly demonstrates [that] the law is defective and needs to be reviewed, particularly in light of legislation applying in Northern Ireland, which would have provided redress in this case.[15]

Interestingly, Carmel Foley of the Employment Equality Agency was more optimistic, observing that "the majority of sexual harassment cases will . . . not be affected since most cases do not involve the extreme sexual violence that occurred in this case."[16] Such a statement, however, might well have been motivated by hope rather than expectation. It would appear more likely that Gary Byrne, the Health Board's solicitor, was correct when he stated that "in future it will be very difficult for plaintiffs — even if they can clearly establish that sexual harassment did occur in the workplace — to establish that this imposes a liability on the employer."[17]

The Effect of the Decision

An individual is generally deemed to be "vicariously liable" when a party under his or her control, acting on his or her behalf, commits a legal wrong.[18] The issue of vicarious liability arises most often in the context of employment relationships where employers can be held vicariously liable for wrongful acts committed by their employees. In this jurisdiction an employer can only be held to be vicariously liable "where the act is committed by his employee within the scope of his employment." As McMahon and Binchy point out:

Press, 20 January 1994. See also "Health board wins appeal on woman's compensation", *The Irish Times*, 20 January 1994.

[15] See "SIPTU call for change in law", *The Cork Examiner*, 21 January 1994.

[16] See Fintan Hourihan, "Change in Law to Follow Landmark Sex Harassment Ruling" (1994) 4 *Industrial Relations News* 17, at *18*.

[17] See Hourihan, *loc. cit., at 18.*

[18] See, generally, McMahon and Binchy, *op. cit.,* at 748 to 768.

It must be realised that the nature of the master/servant relationship, when it exists, has definitional limitations. These limitations may be temporal or spatial. There will, of course, also be
limitations imposed by the nature of the employment and these
we may call functional limitations. . . . The temporal limitation
could mean, for example, that a master would not normally be liable for the torts of a nine-to-five employee committed at 10.00
p.m. or at week-ends. The spatial limitation could mean that the
master would not normally be liable for torts committed by the
servant away from his place of work.[19]

The importance of this spatial limitation has been highlighted by
the courts in both Ireland and England on a number of occasions.[20] In the context of sexual harassment cases it could, for example, preclude a woman who has been visited and harassed at
her home by a fellow employee from succeeding in a claim against
her employer.[21]

In dealing with the functional limitations which are of relevance here McMahon and Binchy cite the test as being that which
was elaborated by Palles C.B.[22] in *Farry v. Great Northern Railway Co.*:

> [T]wo separate things are to be considered: first, the act done;
> secondly, the purpose for which it is done. . . . If the act is outside
> the scope of the servant's employment, the master is not respon-
> sible, and in such a case it is unnecessary to consider the pur-

---

[19] *Op. cit.*, at 755.

[20] See, for example, *Kiely v. McCrea & Sons Ltd.*, [1940] Ir. Jur. Rep. 1, and
the judgment of Lord Lowry in *Smith v. Stages*, [1989] 1 All E.R. 833.

[21] In *A Company v. A Worker*, EEO993, 16 September 1993, the Labour
Court asked itself "whether [an] [e]mployer can be held responsible for an
incident which it is alleged took place in a public place on the way home from
work. The only link with the [e]mployer was that it involved two of his employees. The Court [concluded] that he cannot be responsible for actions
which occur outside the workplace, over which he has no control, and in a
situation where he could not provide protection....However, the Court accepts
that there are occasions when the consequences of such acts could affect
workers in the course of their employment, in that they could cause a dete-
rioration in the working environment. The employer might then acquire a
certain responsibility to the workers affected."

[22] With whom Boyd and Murphy JJ. concurred.

pose. . . . But, when the act . . . is one within the ordinary scope
of the servant's employment then arises the question whether
the act complained of was done *for* the employer; as, if the act,
although of a class within the scope of the employment, was done
by the servant, for his own purposes, such, for instance, as
wreaking his own vengeance or spite upon a particular person,
the act, although capable of being done within the scope of employment, is not in fact done within such scope; it is not done for
the employer.[23]

Palles' *dictum* is particularly interesting in the context of sexual
harassment. If one should, in line with the decision of Costello J.,
apply a test similar to that mapped out by the Chief Baron in the
Farry case,[24] then many victims of sexual harassment who would
in the past have benefited under the rather generous test applied
by the Labour Court, might, post-*B.C.*, find themselves encounter-
ing insurmountable difficulties in proving that their employers
should be held vicariously liable for the acts of their fellow employees. The Department of Equality and Law Reform's *Code of
Practice,*[25] for example, cites as examples of conduct constituting
sexual harassment, *inter alia,* the making of unwelcome sexual
advances, sexually suggestive jokes, remarks or innuendo, unwelcome fondling or kissing, sexual assault or rape.[26] Despite the fact
that all of these forms of conduct undoubtedly constitute sexual
harassment, *per se,* and therefore constitute gender-based discrimination, it is arguable that many of them do not occur "within
the scope of employment" as Palles C.B. defined that term. Any
such argument would certainly be consistent with the decision of
the Court of Appeal in *Aldred v. Nacanco,*[27] wherein the court refused to hold the employer vicariously liable for the actions of an
employee who pushed a washbasin, known to be unsteady,

---

[23] [1898] 2 I.R., at 355-356.

[24] *Loc. cit.*

[25] *Op. cit.*

[26] For a more comprehensive attempt to define sexual harassment see Michael Rubenstein, "What is Sexual Harassment?", (1992) *1 Irish Industrial
Relations Review,* 6.

[27] [1987] I.R.L.R. 292.

against another employee in order to frighten her, on the basis that the actions complained of had nothing to do with anything the aggressor was employed to do, and accordingly, were wholly outside the scope of her employment. Similarly, in *Irving v. Post Office,*[28] the Court of Appeal refused to hold the defendant vicariously liable for the actions of a postman/sorter who wrote an offensive remark on a letter addressed to a couple of Jamaican extraction, as his actions were deemed to be unconnected with the performance of his duties.[29]

In light of the above it would appear that the judgement of Costello J. in the *B.C.* case[30] has severely constricted the utility of the 1977 Act in respect of sexual harassment cases. If employees no longer have access to what McMahon and Binchy refer to as the "deep pocket" of employers in such a wide variety of sexual harassment cases it would seem that the previously attractive avenue of suing employers pursuant to the 1977 Act has, by and large, now been blocked off.

Underestimating the Effect of *B.C.*

In striking at the very heart of the Labour Court's progressive, if somewhat unusual, interpretation of the Employment Equality Act, 1977, Costello J. has not only dramatically curtailed the range of cases in which an employer can be found vicariously liable for acts of sexual harassment perpetrated by his or her employees, but has also stifled, at the early stages of their development, recent and even more liberal developments. In 1991, for example, the Labour Court determined that an employer can be

---

[28] [1987] I.R.L.R. 289.

[29] There is, however, an interesting line of authority which would seem to suggest that employers can, in certain circumstances, be held vicariously liable for criminal acts perpetrated by their employees. That line of authority can be traced back to the House of Lords' decision in *Lloyd v. Grace, Smith & Co.*, [1912] A.C. 716, where the employers of a fraudulent clerk were held liable for his fraud, even though it was never authorised and the company gained no benefit from it. See also *Johnson and Johnson v. C.P. Security,* [1986] I.L.R.M. 559. Unfortunately, it would appear that this line of authority was not explored in the course of the hearing of B.C.'s case. It was certainly not considered by Costello J. in his judgment.

[30] *Op. cit.*

held vicariously liable for the sexual harassment of one of its employees by an individual who is neither an owner nor an employee
of the company in question.[31] It would appear that no such determination could now be reached. Given that such is the case, it
is hardly surprising that attempts have been made both to undermine and to marginalise the importance of Mr. Justice Costello's decision. Academic lawyer Leo Flynn, for example, opted to
attempt to undermine the decision by highlighting a number of
the inconsistencies upon which it was constructed. The result is a
thought-provoking and informative piece.[32] In contrast, Mary
Honan of the Employment Equality Agency has attempted to
marginalise Mr. Justice Costello's decision, effectively arguing
that it is only of relevance in cases which involve sexual assault
or rape.[33] In so doing, Honan would seem to be swimming against
the tide of legal opinion on the effect of the decision in *B.C.*:[34]

> A view has been expressed by some commentators that the High
> Court judgment means that an employer's vicarious liability will
> be very difficult to establish in future cases of alleged discrimi-
> nation generally and in sexual harassment cases in particular.
>   This is very unlikely to be the case since, arguably, most acts
> of discrimination arise within the course of employment, such as
> the discriminatory exercise of functions relating to recruitment,
> promotion, etc. The same should apply to most sexual harass-
> ment cases; these complaints frequently involve abuse or neglect
> of management or supervisory functions, but only rarely sexual
> assault/rape. . . . The judgment would of course affect cases in-

---

[31] *A Worker (SIPTU) v. A Company*, (1992) 3 Employment Law Reports 5.
The Labour Court was willing to hold the company vicariously liable because
the harasser was on the company premises with the agreement of the employer who was in a position to protect the worker. It is, at the very least,
arguable that Palles C.B. would regard such an understanding of the legal
principles underlying the concept of vicarious liability as misguided. For further comment on the case see "Sexual Harassment - Labour Court Awards
£7,500 in Unusual Case", 1992 (3) *Industrial Relations News*. 15.

[32] See Flynn, *loc. cit.*

[33] Mary Honan, "Making Progress in Ireland: Implementing the Code of
Practice on Measures to Protect the Dignity of Women and Men at Work", in
Orla Egan (ed.), *Sexual Harassment at College*, (Cork: UCC, 1995), 15, at 20.

[34] *Op. cit.*

volving sexual assault or rape, but these are rarely dealt with under equality legislation.

In summary, therefore, it is my view that this High Court decision will not have significant impact in practice for either discrimination cases generally or sexual harassment cases in particular.[35]

While the Supreme Court, or even another judge in the High Court, may eventually decide that the decision in *B.C.*[36] should only be relied upon as precedent in cases involving sexual assault or rape, it is more likely that the choice will be whether to disregard the decision on the basis that the legal reasoning involved was flawed or to apply it in all cases involving sexual harassment. The critical point, which Honan would appear either to have overlooked or ignored, is that Mr. Justice Costello held not just that employers could not be held liable for sexual assaults perpetrated by their employees, but, more expansively, that employers could not be held liable for acts perpetrated outside the scope of their employments. If one accepts the approach of Palles C.B. to interpreting the term "scope of employment", then very few acts of sexual harassment can be deemed to be perpetrated within the scope of individuals' employments as only a tiny percentage of such acts are done *for* employers. For that reason, Honan's assessment of the impact of the decision in *B.C.* would seem to be misleading.

In an attempt to bolster her argument, Honan refers to a "decision made by the Labour Court some months after" Costello J. handed down his decision in *B.C.*[37] In the case in question, a "waitress alleged that she had been sexually harassed and victimised by a head chef, until she had no alternative but to leave her

---

[35] Honan, *loc. cit.* See also "Sexual Harassment after *BC v. MHB*", (1995) 3 *Equality News* 12, wherein Honan repeats her argument.

[36] *Op. cit.*

[37] EEO 2/94. See Honan, "Making Progress in Ireland: Implementing the Code of Practice on Measures to Protect the Dignity of Women and Men at Work", *loc. cit.*, at 20; and Honan, "Sexual Harassment after *BC v. MHB*", *loc. cit.*, at 12.

employment."[38] The employer relied on the decision given in
B.C.,[39] arguing that the acts complained of did not come within
the scope of the harasser's employment. The Court, surprisingly,
made no real attempt to come to terms with the guidelines
mapped out by Mr. Justice Costello earlier that year. Rather, it
found the employer liable, opining that the head chef "had control
over what occurred in the workplace, and that control had been
given to him by the company. The company must, therefore, take
responsibility if he abuses his position of power."

While the Labour Court's decision would appear to be more
consistent with the intention behind, and terms of, the Employment Equality Act, 1977, than that of Costello J. in the earlier
case, it cannot seriously be argued that the Court's decision was
in any way defensible. It is clearly the case that any judgment of
the High Court is binding on the Labour Court. In this case, the
Labour Court clearly chose to ignore that fact. In that context, one
simply cannot rely on the Labour Court's decision in an attempt
to argue that the precedent created by Mr. Justice Costello has
very limited application.

Gaps in the Logic of the Decision

While, as has been pointed out above, Mr. Justice Costello's decision is arguably consistent with a number of previous judgments
in cases concerning the vicarious liability of employers for the
acts of their employees, there are two specific points in the judgment which deserve further consideration. In respect of both
points Mr. Justice Costello's decision is open to criticism and, it
will be suggested, might have been reversible on appeal.

The first, and less important, of the two points is that Costello
J. patently failed to deal with the issue of the Health Board's potential liability in respect of the harassers' conduct in the period
leading up to the assault on 18 November 1989. It is clear from
the text of the judgment that Costello J. regarded that conduct,
which included the uttering of "lewd and course" remarks and
non-consensual touching, as constituting sexual harassment and,

---

[38] Employment Equality Agency, Annual Report, 1994, (Dublin, 1995), at 19.

[39] *Op. cit.*

for that reason, "discrimination" within the meaning of the 1977 Act. After going on to consider and determine the nature of the Health Board's liability for the assault of 18 November, however, Costello J. failed to return to the earlier acts of harassment on the part of B.C.'s fellow employees. It is submitted that these earlier acts might have been construed at common law as having come within the scope of the harassers' employments.[40]

The second weakness in Costello's judgment is arguably that his strict, black-letter application of common law principles contrasts starkly with the intent of the legislature in enacting the Employment Equality Act, 1977, at least in so far as the spirit of the legislature's intentions has been interpreted by both the Labour Court and industrial relations practitioners. Before expanding on this idea one must first point out that the claim that sexual harassment constitutes "discrimination" within the meaning of the 1977 Act would seem to be unquestionable. Costello J. himself seems to have accepted the validity of the Labour Court's analysis of the Act in that respect. If such is the case and one also accepts that the legislature intended, in enacting the 1977 legislation, to tackle the problem of discrimination in the workplace then one must surely also accept that the legislature intended to impose liability on employers. If that was not the intention then the 1977 Act can be little more than a toothless watchdog.

The decision of the Supreme Court of Canada in *Robichaud v. R.*[41] provides some considerable guidance on this point. Human rights legislation in Canada does not expressly impose liability on employers for acts of sexual harassment perpetrated by their employees. For that reason, Canadian tribunals have effectively been compelled to explore, in some considerable detail, the common law position in relation to the matter. From an early stage it became clear that Canadian tribunals had every intention of en-

---

[40] See McMahon and Binchy, *op. cit.*, at 757-758. See also *Harrison v. Michelin Tyre Co. Ltd.*, [1985] 1 All E.R. 918, and *Hough v. Irish Base Metals Ltd.*, unreported, Supreme Court, 8 December 1967.

[41] [1987] 2 S.C. R. 84, 40 D.L.R. (4th) 577.

suring that liability would attach to employers.[42] According to Aggarwal:

> [p]rior to the Supreme Court decision in *Robichaud v. R.*,[43] the Human Rights Tribunals had to go through various legal gymnastics to find that the employer is liable for the discriminatory conduct of their employees, though without any certainty that their findings would be upheld by the higher courts. . . .[44]

In *Robichaud*,[45] the Federal Court of Appeal delivered a judgment which was even more restrictive than that of Costello J. in *The Health Board v. B.C.*[46] In what Aggarwal describes as a "devastating" decision,[47] the Court held that only the person who actually committed a discriminatory act (in this case, an act constituting sexual harassment) could be held liable under the legislation. Dramatically, however, the Supreme Court completely overturned the decision of the Court of Appeal[48] and, in doing so, clearly mapped out the ambit of employers' liability in respect of discriminatory acts perpetrated by employees. The Court pointed out that the rules attaching to the concept of "vicarious liability", as it existed in tort law, could not "meaningfully be applied to the . . . statutory scheme" because of their restrictive limitation to acts occurring in the course, or within the scope, of employment. Any attempt to strictly apply those rules, the court held, would

---

[42] See Arjun P. Aggarwal, *Sexual Harassment in the Workplace*, 2nd ed., (Toronto: Butterworths, 1992), 181 *et seq.*

[43] *Op. cit.*

[44] Aggarwal, *op. cit.*, at 189-190.

[45] *Op. cit.*

[46] *Op. cit.*

[47] Aggarwal, *op. cit.*, at 193.

[48] That they should do so came as no great surprise to those who are familiar with the history of the Canadian Supreme Court. As Catharine McKinnon has pointed out, the "Supreme Court of Canada is the first court in the world to adopt the reality of social disadvantage as a basis for constitutional analysis. It will as a result, be the first court which will have the opportunity to change these inequalities." As quoted in K. Mahoney, "The Constitutional Law of Equality in Canada", 24 *Int. Law and Politics* 759, at 793.

merely serve to stultify the remedial objectives of the statute.[49] Rather, it was felt, any legitimate interpretation of the Act had to recognise that Parliament had, in legislating on the matter, been attempting to give effect to the principle of equal opportunity for individuals by eradicating invidious discrimination. Such an eradication of discrimination would be far more difficult to achieve, the Court added, if the remedies enumerated in the Act were not available against employers as only employers could order reinstatement, compensate for lost wages and provide healthy work environments. In concluding its decision the Court refused to attempt to definitively categorise the nature of the employer's liability. Such liability, it held, was purely statutory and did not require any label.

Reasoning similar to that of the Canadian Supreme Court's has also been employed on this side of the Atlantic. In the Scottish case of *Strathclyde Regional Council v. Porcelli*[50] the Lord President of the Court of Session expressed the view that sexual harassment is a "particularly degrading and unacceptable form of treatment which it must be taken to be the intention of Parliament to restrain."[51] Of the two cases, however, *Robichaud* must be regarded as the better precedent, given the Court's detailed consideration of the matter and the fact that the decision was handed down by a Court of supreme jurisdiction.

In 1988, one year after the Canadian Supreme Court handed down its decision in Robichaud, Irish Equality Officer, Margaret Monaghan, applied similar logic in arriving at an almost identical decision in *A Limited Company v. One Female Employee*.[52] Showing a wonderful appreciation of the legal subtleties involved in the matter, Ms. Monaghan concluded that:

> [T]he common law doctrine of vicarious liability . . . has no relevance to discriminatory acts by senior management contrary to the Employment Equality Act, 1977. This is clear from the test in

---

[49] The Canadian Human Rights Act.

[50] [1986] I.R.L.R. 400.

[51] *Ibid.*, at 137.

[52] EE10/1988; 30 December 1988.

MacMahon & Binchy's *Irish Law of Torts* . . . that test being "whether the act in question was within the scope of the servant's duties." In a very real sense an act of sexual harassment by its nature could never be deemed to be within the scope of the servant's duties.

Equally, the passage quoted from p.107 of MacMahon & Binchy would totally defeat the objective of the Employment Equality Act if it were to be applied to discrimination by way of sexual harassment. If any senior employee of a limited liability company was deemed to be "on a frolic of his own" when he engaged in sexual harassment of other employees of the company, then a limited liability employer could never be found to discriminate by way of sexual harassment although an individual employer clearly would be found so liable in similar circumstances. No distinction is drawn in the Act between individual and limited liability employers and to seek to import the common law doctrine . . . would be to defeat the clear intention of the Oireachtas and the objective of the Employment Equality Act, 1977.

It is submitted that the decision in *Robichaud*[53] might well be regarded as the ideal blueprint for the courts in this jurisdiction to follow in the future. As Mr. Justice Costello quite devastatingly illustrated in *The Health Board v. B.C.*[54] the old common law principles relating to vicarious liability (especially if applied in a manner consistent with the decision in *Farry*[55]) are not flexible enough to be able to plug what is unquestionably a glaring gap in the legislative response to gender-based discrimination in the workplace. It is, however, quite clear that the legislature intended, in enacting the legislation in question, to comprehensively tackle such discrimination.[56] In interpreting the Act as

---

[53] *Op. cit.*

[54] *Op. cit.*

[55] *Op. cit.*

[56] In the case of *An Blascaod Mór Teo v. Commissioners of Public Works in Ireland and Others*, Unreported, High Court, 27 November 1992, Murphy J. opined that, in legal terms, an analysis of the motivation of the Oireachtas in enacting legislation would be meaningless in practice and wholly unwarranted by the doctrine of the separation of powers. That *dictum*, however, would appear to be at odds with a number of earlier decisions. For an inter-

narrowly as he has done, Costello J. might well be accused of effectively rendering it impotent insofar as it deals with the issue of workplace sexual harassment. Instead of blindly following Mr. Justice Costello into that trap in the future, it is to be hoped that the courts will see the route around it already mapped out by their Canadian brethren.

Legislative Reform

It would seem that Mr. Justice Costello's decision is more likely to be countered in Leinster House than in the Four Courts as Mervyn Taylor, TD, Minister for Equality and Law Reform, has promised to introduce legislation dealing expressly with sexual harassment. In his address to a conference organised by the Employment Equality Agency in 1993 the Minister stated that:

> While the present legislation has served us well, I am currently reviewing the existing employment equality legislation in line with the commitment in the Programme for a Partnership Government to introduce more explicit provisions in relation to sexual harassment. Furthermore, I am looking closely at the question of making employers vicariously liable for consistent harassment which might take place on their premises or in the course of their employment.[57]

In commenting on the decision in *The Health Board v. B.C.*,[58] the Minister once again promised that the issue of sexual harassment would be addressed in his draft Bill, and pointed out that he would consider what alterations might be necessary after the handing down of Mr. Justice Costello's decision.[59]

Given the Minister's track record of delivering on his promises it would seem that the portents are good for those who wish to see the effect of Mr. Justice Costello's decision reversed by the legisla-

---

esting analysis of the matter see Raymond Byrne and William Binchy, *Annual Review of Irish Law 1992* (Dublin: Round Hall Press, 1994), at 139-141.

[57] Mervyn Taylor, TD, Minister for Equality and Law Reform, in an address to the Employment Equality Agency's Conference on Sexual Harassment in the Workplace, "Making Advances", Dublin Castle, 15 October 1993.

[58] *Op. cit.*

[59] See "Sex harassment case causes concern", *The Evening Press,* 20 January 1994.

ture. While such a development would, almost certainly, be criticised by organisations representing employers, it is very probable
that it would serve to limit the number of occasions on which
working women are subjected to sexual harassment by their fellow employees. At the very least it would ensure that women such
as B.C. are not denied legal redress in the future.

Employers' Defences[60]

In the wake of Mr. Justice Costello's decision in the *B.C.* case,[61] it
would seem that employers seeking to avoid being held liable for
acts of sexual harassment perpetrated by their employees will, for
the foreseeable future, at least, argue initially that their employees were not acting "within the scope of their employment" when
they committed the acts complained of. As has already been explained, that line of argument would appear to have considerable
potential for employers if they can persuade the courts that employees are only acting "within the scope of their employment"
when they are acting in a manner which is likely to benefit their
employers.

There is, however, a second defence which has been successfully raised by employers on a number of occasions in both Ireland and the United Kingdom. That defence involves the employer relying upon the fact that he or she has implemented and
enforced an adequate sexual harassment policy and complaints
procedure. As the equality officer explained in her determination
in *An Employer v. One Female Employee:*

> . . . if the employer took all reasonable practicable steps to ensure
> that each of its employees enjoyed working conditions, free from
> sexual harassment, the discrimination carried out by its two
> male employees would not constitute a contravention by the
> employer of section 3.[62]

---

[60] See also Chapter Seven.

[61] *Op. cit.*

[62] *Per* Deirdre Sweeney, Equality Officer, in *An Employer v. One Female
Employee*, EE22/1991, 4 November 1991.

This second defence has been recognised by the Labour Court for some years. For that reason, both the Employment Equality Agency and IBEC provide advice on the questions of sexual harassment policies and complaints procedures. Those matters are also dealt with in Chapters Four and Five.

REMEDIES

The Employment Equality Act, 1977, provides victims of sex discrimination with only one possible remedy against their employers — that of compensation up to a maximum of the equivalent of two years remuneration. Section 23(a) of the Act provides that the Court may:

> award to the plaintiff a sum not exceeding such amount as in the opinion of the court the plaintiff would have received from the person against whom the determination was made by way of damages in respect of remuneration in relation to the matter the subject of the determination, but not in any case exceeding 104 weeks' remuneration.

While section 23(a) is similar in effect to that which pertained in Britain until recently, it is substantially dissimilar to provisions contained in legislation in a number of other jurisdictions. In most Canadian provinces, for example, human rights statutes authorise the court, tribunal or board of inquiry in question to "rectify any injury caused to any person and to make compensation."[63] Adjudicating bodies have, for that reason, broad powers to award any number of discretionary remedies. In America, the Courts also have wide discretionary powers. Section 706(9) of the US Civil Rights Act, 1964, empowers courts to issue prohibitory injunctions forbidding discriminatory practices as well as mandatory injunctions requiring employers to take

> such affirmative action as may be appropriate, which may include but is not limited to reinstatement or hiring of employees with or without backpay . . . or any other equitable relief as the court may deem appropriate.

---

[63] Aggarwal, *op. cit.*, at 243.

While American awards of damages have been criticised in this country as being excessive, it is worth noting that the US Supreme Court has made it clear that the deterrent effect of the possibility of large awards in sex discrimination cases is meant to spur employers to eliminate discriminatory practices on their own initiative.[64] As Deirdre Curtin has explained:

> In both the Irish and British equality legislation the potent arsenal of remedies needed to enable the courts to give practical effect to the concepts enshrined in the equality legislation is missing. £1,000 compensation will not make a victim of discrimination, forced to quit her job, whole. If sexual harassment in employment is to be remedied and deterred, comprehensive remedies tailored to the injuries suffered by victims are essential. It is necessary that the full spectrum of tort damages as well as equitable relief should be made available.[65]

Due in large part to the statutory ceiling on damages in Ireland, the Labour Court has, thus far, been limited to awarding what Curtin has, quite rightly, referred to as "derisory" sums to victims of sexual harassment.[66] The statutory limit has not, however, been the only factor preventing the Labour Court from awarding substantial damages. The Court has, quite intentionally, restrained itself in assessing damages in sex discrimination cases. In *Smith v. C.I.E.* the Court claimed that "the statutory maximum . . . should be reserved for the very worst type of discrimination falling within the definition and that regard should be had

---

[64] *Albermale Paper Co. v. Moody*, (1975) 422 U.S. 405.

[65] Deirdre Curtin, "Sexual Harassment in Employment - Developing a Standard of Employer Liability", (1984) 6 *Dublin University Law Journal* (n.s.) 75, 87.

[66] Curtin, *loc. cit.*, at 86. It would seem that the Employment Equality Agency is also dissatisfied with the *quantum* of awards. In 1991, the then Chief Executive of the Employment Equality Agency, Sylvia Meehan, stated that "awards in sexual harassment cases should be made by reference to the fact of discrimination itself, once this established, and also by reference to the loss of opportunity and the trauma suffered by claimants. . . . " In determining the size of awards, Ms. Meehan said that the Labour Court should also take account of the loss of potential future earnings suffered by a woman who is forced to leave her job as a result of sexual harassment. *The Irish Times,* 11 January 1991.

to this in deciding lesser amounts."[67] In *A Company v. A Worker*[68] the claimant was, *inter alia,*

> subjected to advances of a sexual and intimidating nature and put under pressure to socialise. She stated she was subjected to offensive language, crude jokes, details of sexual experiences and to frequent phone calls to her home in the evenings and at weekends."

The claimant was eventually left with no option other than to resign from her job as an area sales manager and was diagnosed by her doctor as suffering from debilitating stress. Quite remarkably, the Labour Court awarded her a mere £2,500; less than one-seventh of a year's salary. Given relatively recent developments in the European Court of Justice, however, it would appear that the Labour Court should no longer be attempting to steer by a maximum. In *Marshall v. Southampton and South West Hampshire Area Health Authority (Teaching), No. 2,*[69] the Court of Justice held that Ms. Marshall could rely directly on the provisions of Article 6 of Council Directive 76/207/EEC[70] in order to set aside a national provision which limited the amount of money recoverable by her as compensation for the discriminatory treatment she had suffered.

Ms. Marshall was a senior dietician employed by the Southampton and South West District Area Health Authority from July 1966 to 31 March 1980. At the age of 62 she was dismissed on the ground that she had passed the normal retirement age for women, which was 60, at which age women were entitled to a State pension. Ms. Marshall sued the Health Authority under the

---

[67] EE 4/1979, DEE 1/1979.

[68] EEO692.

[69] Case C-271/91, ECJ judgment of 2 August 1993.

[70] Council Directive 76/207/EEC of 9 February, 1976 (Official Journal 1976 L 39, p.40). Article 6 provides that "Member States shall introduce into their national legal systems such measures as are necessary to enable all persons who consider themselves wronged by failure to apply to them the principle of equal treatment within the meaning of Articles 3, 4 and 5 to pursue their claims by judicial process after possible recourse to other competent authorities."

U.K. Sex Discrimination Act, 1975, and won. Section 65(2) of that Act, however, imposed an upper limit of £6,250 on the amount of compensation recoverable by claimants. In 1991, the House of Lords referred the matter to the European Court of Justice which held that

> [a] person who has been injured as a result of discriminatory dismissal may rely on the provisions of Article 6 of the Directive as against an authority of the State acting in its capacity as an employer in order to set aside a national provision which imposes limits on the amount of compensation recoverable by way of reparation."

The principles underpinning the decision of the Court of Justice's decision do not apply simply to discriminatory dismissals. Rather, they would seem to apply to all incidents of discrimination, including sexual harassment.

The Conservative Government in Britain quickly responded to the decision, introducing the Sex Discrimination and Equal Pay (Remedies) Regulations, 1993,[71] which abolished the ceiling on awards of compensation imposed by the 1975 Act.[72] While Ireland was represented at the *Marshall* hearing before the European Court of Justice, no similar measures have been introduced in this jurisdiction. Irish claimants can, nevertheless, rely directly on Article 6 of the Directive in seeking damages in excess of those provided for in the 1977 Act. In light of the increased levels of compensation being awarded to victims of sex discrimination in the UK since the Court of Justice handed down its decision in Marshall, it would appear that those who rely on Article 6 in this jurisdiction could be awarded sums far greater than those provided for under the 1977 Act.

Figure 3.1 sums up the key points on employers' liability, defences and remedies.

---

[71] SI93/2798.

[72] See "Interest in sex", (1993) *New Law Journal* 1778.

Figure 3.1: Employers Liability, Defences and Remedies

"The law is sometimes prepared to hold one person liable for the wrong committed by another person even though the person held liable is not at fault in the accepted sense of the word. Thus the law may hold the master liable for the wrongs of his servant . . . in spite of the fact that the master . . . may not have been at fault in any way . . . ." — McMahon and Binchy, *op. cit.*, at 748.

"In the absence of express statutory provision the law in this country in relation to the liability of an employee for the tortious acts (including statutory torts) of his employee is perfectly clear - an employer is vicariously liable where the act is committed within the scope of his employment. . . . An employer may, of course, be vicariously liable when his employee is acting negligently, or even criminally. . . . But I cannot envisage any employment in which they were engaged in respect of which a sexual assault could be regarded as so connected with it as to amount to an act within its scope." — Costello J., *The Health Board v. B.C. and the Labour Court, op. cit.*

"[T]wo separate things are to be considered: first, the act done; secondly, the purpose for which it is done. . . . If the act is outside the scope of the servant's employment, the master is not responsible, and in such a case it is unnecessary to consider the purpose. . . . But, when the act . . . is one within the ordinary scope of the servant's employment then arises the question whether the act complained of was done for the employer; as, if the act, although of a class within the scope of the employment, was done by the servant, for his own purposes, such, for instance, as wreaking his own vengeance or spite upon a particular person, the act, although capable of being done within the scope of employment, is not in fact done within such scope; it is not done for the employer." — Palles C.B., *Farry v. Great Northern Railway Co., op. cit.*

"[T]he common law doctrine of vicarious liability . . . has no relevance to discriminatory acts by senior management contrary to the Employment Equality Act, 1977. This is clear from the test in MacMahon & Binchy's *Irish Law of Torts* . . . that test being "whether the act in question was within the scope of the servant's duties." In a very real sense an act of sexual harassment by its nature could never be deemed to be within the scope of the servant's duties." — Margaret Monaghan, Equality Officer, EE10/1988.

"I am looking closely at the question of making employers vicariously liable for consistent harassment which might take place on their premises or in the course of their employment."— Mervyn Taylor, TD, Minister for Equality and Law Reform, *op. cit.*

"[I]f the employer took all reasonable practicable steps to ensure that each of its employees enjoyed working conditions, free from sexual harassment, the discrimination carried out by its two male employees would not constitute a contravention by the employer of section 3." — Deirdre Sweeney, Equality Officer, in *An Employer v. One Female Employee*, EE22/1991.

CHAPTER FOUR

SEXUAL HARASSMENT POLICIES: AN EFFECTIVE EMPLOYER STRATEGY

The creation of a climate to challenge harassment begins with [the generation of a] policy. A firm, unequivocal statement from the top that harassment is totally unacceptable sends a clear message throughout the organisation.[1]

INTRODUCTION

Sexual harassment is as likely to occur in large firms as it is in small ones. Even within firms, sexual harassment affects everyone. No group of people, or particular profession, is characterised by an absence of sexual harassment. As MacKinnon has explained:

> Victimisation by the practice of sexual harassment, so far as is currently known, occurs across the lines of age, marital status, physical appearance, race, class, occupation, pay range, and any other factor that distinguishes women from each other. Frequency and type of incident may vary with specific vulnerabilities of the woman, or qualities of the job, employer, situation, or workplace, to an extent so far undetermined. To this point, the common denominator is that the perpetrators tend to be men, the victims women. [2]

That having been said, the Irish Bank Officials' Association (IBOA) have quite correctly pointed out that:

---

[1] Kerry Hawkins, "Taking Action on Harassment," *Personnel Management*, March 1994, 26, at 26.

[2] Catharine A. MacKinnon. *Sexual Harassment of Working Women: A Case of Sex Discrimination* (New Haven and London: Yale University Press, 1979), 28.

certain sectors [of] the workforce are more vulnerable to sexual harassment than others; for example, young employees, new entrants, temporary and part time employees, disabled employees and workers in non-traditional jobs". [3]

As was explained in Chapter One, the consequences of sexual harassment for the victim are immense. They can include low productivity, low self esteem and possible resignation from the company. Employers will also suffer as a result of low productivity, the loss of good employees and the cost of replacing those who resign and re-training others.

Another reason for employer concern relates to the costs of being sued. An individual who has been harassed can take a case to the Labour Court. Such cases are clearly bad publicity for the company. The likelihood of losing a case in the Labour Court is increased for a firm that lacks a well defined policy on sexual harassment. Further, if a company — or rather a manager or supervisor as representatives of the company — knew about the problem and did little to counteract it, the employer could very well be held responsible. Clearly, an employer should do something about sexual harassment — preferably limiting the possibility of harassment happening in the first place.

Some might argue that the employer has a duty to uphold the law and little more. It is submitted that such a minimalist approach is not enough. Rather, the employer must approach the issue of sexual harassment from the standpoint of employment equality and develop a proactive stance which is designed to achieve firstly, a harassment-free environment, and secondly, an environment which is supportive of women's rights at work. The ESB is, perhaps, the leading example of an Irish firm in this regard, having an excellent record on employment equality issues and having gone far beyond what the law currently requires at present.

This chapter, taking its cue from the ESB and other similar organisations, is based on a proactive approach. Proactive means taking a stance which stops sexual harassment before it happens

---

[3] Irish Bank Officials Association, "Sexual Harassment Policy", (Dublin: IBOA, undated).

and which places sexual harassment at the centre of a co-ordinated and structured approach to the issue of employment equality. The fact that the material for this chapter is drawn from large organisations should not, however, deter smaller companies from adopting similar, if not identical, procedures.

CURRENT EMPLOYER STRATEGY ON SEXUAL HARASSMENT

Some organisations have made a concerted effort to combat sexual harassment, while others have done little or nothing. More likely to fall into the former category are large organisations, particularly those in the public sector. Small and non-union firms are less likely to have policies. Hence, despite repeated announcements from IBEC and the EEA that firms should adopt sexual harassment policies, few organisations have done so. The EEA, for example, "strongly recommends":

1. The issuing of a policy statement by employers (in consultation where appropriate with the trade union) condemning sexual harassment.

2. The inclusion of procedures for dealing with sexual harassment in grievance and disciplinary procedures. Any clause dealing with sexual harassment should provide for prompt action.[4]

Though it has both a commitment and a record to date of taking cases to the Labour Court on behalf on individuals, the EEA maintains that sexual harassment is best dealt with at the level of the workplace, with a co-ordinated policy in place. In other words, complaints should be dealt with at the source, under the premise that prevention is better than cure. IBEC have taken a similar view adding that once a policy is in place, a firm should provide extra training in the area of sexual harassment and organise meetings so as to communicate that policy to the workforce. Finally, ICTU has called on its member unions to negotiate policies on sexual harassment and include these within general policies on employment equality. In addition, ICTU has advised

---

[4] Employment Equality Agency, *Equality at Work: Sexual Harassment* (Dublin: EEA, undated).

unions to regularly inform members about sexual harassment, and to provide support for members who wish to make complaints.

Thus, there is pressure from a government agency, the largest employer's organisation, and the congress of trade unions to encourage firms to adopt policies on sexual harassment. The views of IBEC, ICTU and indeed the EEA are reflected in the Irish Code of Practice, which encourages, but does not mandate, firms to implement sexual harassment policies.[5] Despite all of this, as already noted, few organisations have implemented policies.[6]

The Advantages of a Sexual Harassment Policy

Aside from being informative, a sexual harassment policy helps employers to deal with the issue of sexual harassment, as well providing themselves with a measure of legal protection. If taken to court over the issue of sexual harassment, an employer can always point to a policy document as partial evidence that he or she is taking steps to minimise the problem.

Aside from legal reasons, which are important in themselves, it is also good management practice to have a policy. Employees cannot be expected to work without proper protection, no more than managers cannot manage without proper guidelines. Finally, without a policy, employees, as Rubenstein notes,[7] are more likely to seek redress for sexual harassment in the Labour Court than internally.

Sexual harassment polices are not costly to design and operate. They will neither prevent someone from joining a firm, nor take the social element out of work. Men and women can continue to work together, joking, mixing, and enjoying each other's company.

---

[5] See Appendix I.

[6] Margaret Nolan, Training and Equality Officer with ICTU, makes a relevant point "(P)rogress on negotiating workplace agreements has been very uneven — the vast majority are in the public sector, with the private sector lagging far behind". Nolan, "Trade Union Strategies and Initiatives For Dealing With Sexual Harassment", paper delivered to the EEA Conference on Sexual Harassment, 15 October 1993.

[7] Michael Rubenstein, *Preventing and Remedying Sexual Harassment at Work, A Resource Manual*. Industrial Relations Service, 19.

A policy which is well-formulated should not infringe on people's rights to enjoy normal, consensual relationships. Some employees may feel perturbed by a policy, seeing it as an unnecessary intrusion into their private lives. Some may feel that the issue is overblown, that a policy is counter-productive or unnecessary, and some may be, genuinely or otherwise, offended by them. These individuals will, however, be in the minority, and their numbers will become fewer over the years as more and more policies are put in place, and the more people come to accept the need for them.

ESB Strategy

As noted, the ESB has taken a strong stand against sexual harassment.[8] They have a well staffed and well financed unit whose overall responsibility is the promotion of employment equality in the company. Specific to sexual harassment, this unit has, in conjunction with the various trade unions (particularly the ESB Officers Association), devised a policy on sexual harassment. Sexual harassment, in the ESB, is defined as follows:

> Conduct of a sexual nature or conduct based on sex which is offensive to the recipient. It is behaviour that is unwanted, unsolicited, personally offensive and fails to respect the rights of others. It does not refer to behaviour of a flirtatious or romantic nature which is freely or mutually entered into.

The definition thus clarifies what sexual harassment is (offensive, unwanted, unsolicited behaviour) and what it is not (behaviour freely entered into). Bearing in mind that the ESB circulates this policy to all its 9,000-plus staff, and have conducted extensive training programmes using the Dublin Rape Crisis Centre, there can be no excuse for any ESB employee saying that he or she does not know what sexual harassment is.

---

[8] The information in this passage is gained from a number of ESB publications and with interviews with ESB personnel and union officials. The relevant publications are; "Company Policy Regarding Sexual Harassment"; "Guidelines for Managers and Supervisors When Investigating An Allegation of Sexual Harassment"; and "Who Can I Tell: Sexual Harassment Support Colleagues". These are issued to all ESB staff by the ESB Equal Opportunities Office based in the ESB headquarters in Dublin.

Secondly, there is a statement confirming employees' right to a harassment-free environment:

> The ESB wants to ensure that its work environment gives all employees the freedom to do their work free from the threat of sexual harassment.

Thirdly, the ESB has made it obligatory on the part of all supervisors and managers to deal directly with any complaint of sexual harassment. This helps to ensure consistency across the company, as well as to raise awareness of the issue. Hence:

> Each and every staff member has a duty to ensure that sexual harassment does not occur at any level in the company. Management have a special responsibility to ensure this. When a person comes to you wishing to lodge a grievance or complaint of sexual harassment, start by assuring them that you take the complaint seriously and that action will be taken quickly and discreetly. Be aware of the difficulties for the complainant i.e. embarrassment, fear of the outcome, etc. Ascertain the facts, express no opinion and make no commitment. Put aside your personal biases and allow the person to speak candidly. Encourage the complainant to clarify precisely what happened.

The policy, which was adopted in 1988, has not been changed. However, there have been additions to it. Conscious of the fact that few complaints of sexual harassment were being made, the ESB introduced an extension of the programme in 1995.[9] Basically, this extension entailed having a person (support colleague) in each district who could, if necessary, be the point of first contact for an individual who needs advice and support on sexual harassment. The names of these people — all volunteers who were trained by the Dublin Rape Crisis Centre — are listed on an ESB brochure circulated to staff in early 1995. As a victims' support network it is designed both to raise awareness of the issue, as well as to provide an alternative and more meaningful route for people to make complaints. The programme is aimed primarily at the victim — a harasser can ring any of these people, but he

---

[9] ESB, "Who Can I Tell: Sexual Harassment Support Colleagues" (Dublin: ESB, 1995).

will be referred to someone else. However, a supervisor can utilise this network to obtain advice on how to handle a sexual harassment complaint.

The unions were not directly involved in this process, though they would have been aware of it through a union-management committee. The ESBOA, who represent the bulk of female employees, especially clerical staff, in the ESB, has been critical of this lack of involvement. Paul Ennis, Equal Opportunities Manager in the ESB, is adamant that sexual harassment is part of the overall management responsibility to manage. In Ennis's view, their policy is "management-driven because it is a management policy. The ownership of the problem lies with management". Undertaking that policy means engendering a culture in which employees have a responsibility to themselves and to others not to offend a fellow employee. Supervisors have a particular responsibility to address sexual harassment, especially in handling complaints. This, to Ennis, is not an industrial relations issue. However, the company's policy is to involve and consult with the unions, though not necessarily co-determine (that is, seek union agreement before an action becomes policy). Ennis was of the opinion that, despite this criticism from the ESBOA, and despite the special role afforded to first line managers, there has not been any backlash from the unions or from staff. Most employees, in his view, support ESB policy on sexual harassment.

The ESBOA's criticism of this network, it should be noted, relates only to the lack of union involvement, and the fact that, as the union claims, the network involves too many managers and not enough blue-collar employees and clerical staff. According to the ESB, most of the support colleagues are middle level managers, but there are also some electricians and clerical officers, as well as a worker director. Two-thirds are women. This criticism aside, the ESBOA is fully supportive of the ESB. The union participates on a joint union-management committee (Joint Equality Council) which oversees the operation of employment equality policy in the ESB. The Equal Opportunities Office has a very good working relationship with the ESBOA, a point confirmed by both Ennis and the union.

The main incidences of sexual harassment with which the ESB have dealt to date are lewd jokes, offensive pictures and touching. Ennis found that in talking with female employees most regarded harassment "as a damn nuisance". As such, they preferred to have it dealt with in an informal way by having the harasser told to stop. The victim's supervisor would typically do that. The informal approach seems to work. The ESB has not had any serious incident of sexual harassment, nor has the company ever conducted an investigation or had to answer a claim in the Labour Court. Despite the preference for handling complaints informally, the ESB are prepared to go all the way with a complaint, if necessary. For confidential reasons, the ESB does not keep check on the number of complaints it handles. However, Ennis pointed out that the number of complaints, formal and informal, were very small. The ESB has not had any malicious claims, though they did deal with one case of harassment based on sexual orientation. Finally, the ESB is examining the issue of harassment by customers of ESB employees. Its response is likely to take the form of posting a notice in shops asking customers to respect the integrity of shop assistants.

More broadly, the ESB has a proactive employment equality policy. Recently, they implemented a programme aimed at enabling women in clerical positions to become electricians. They also do a lot of work in schools and have solicited applications from women for apprenticeship training. This year they will implement a new code of practice for people with disabilities, and are further extending their policy on job-sharing. According to Ennis, the ESB is well aware that they are in a fortunate position. Being a large company they have the resources to have a designated equal opportunities office and to be proactive. His advice for other companies, especially small ones, is that it is imperative for at least one manager, if not the managing director, to adopt a personal approach to the issue. Put simply, someone has to take the lead and make it known to all employees that sexual harassment won't be tolerated and that action will be taken against any individual who harasses another.

AN EFFECTIVE STRATEGY: SOME GENERAL GUIDELINES

As can be gathered from the example of the ESB, there is much an employer can do to deal with the problem of sexual harassment.[10]

The first step is to recognise the need for a policy on the issue. The employer must recognise the seriousness of the problem, not just the cost to individuals but also the way these costs carry over to the employer in terms of lower productivity and low staff morale. It also means having an employment equality policy with the elimination, or at least minimisation, of sexual harassment as its goal. An employer must remember that he or she has an important duty to employees — namely, to provide a safe work environment.

Secondly, an employer should be fully aware of what sexual harassment is and should communicate it to all staff. Sexual harassment was defined and explained in Chapter One, but it is worth reiterating in brief here some pertinent points that employers should be aware of:

- An employer should not assume that sexual harassment is something which only affects women. Men can be harassed as well, and women can be harassed by other women.

- An employer should not assume that the alleged harasser is the supervisor of a worker. A co-worker, even one in a subordinate position, can do it. So can a customer, or any other non-employee of the firm, such as a delivery person.

- Sexual harassment is not always the outcome of a particular incident or incidents. It can, rather, be caused by an atmosphere, not a person. The hanging of pornographic pictures, the constant telling of dirty jokes or the use of foul language can

---

[10] Much of the advice given in this and other chapters relates to large organisations. As the *Code of Practice*, states (page 7): "The recommendations should be applied in a way which is appropriate to the individual employment. In particular, small and medium-sized organisations may need to adapt the procedures recommended". Department of Equality and Law Reform, *Code of Practice: Measures to Protect the Dignity of Women and Men at Work*. (Dublin, 1994), 17.

create an atmosphere which demeans employees and undermines their ability to perform their jobs. The employer should
not be reluctant to tackle problems of this kind.

- Sexual harassment affects different people in different ways.
  Indeed, the person who makes a complaint may not be the one
  whom the harassment is directed at. An organisation therefore
  has to be aware of the peculiarities of sexual harassment and
  that the law judges the recipient's reaction, not the harasser's
  intention. Therefore, a policy has to be framed in broad and
  encompassing terms, and be legally and factually correct.

Thirdly, the employer should recognise that prevention is the key
to a successful sexual harassment policy. For this reason, employees and their representative should be involved in, or at least informed about, the design and implementation of the policy. In
terms of content, policies should express strong disapproval of the
issue and outline in clear language the procedures and disciplinary measures for dealing with it. Central to dealing with the latter is — following the lead of the ESB — the question of making
managers and supervisors responsible for preventing sexual harassment. All employees should, however, be informed as to their
roles in maintaining a harassment-free environment. Any policy
that is well-formulated should be encouraging rather than intimidating, and it should, ideally, lead to fewer incidents of sexual
harassment. A policy gains little respect unless it is implemented
and administered properly. It gains even less respect when employees have had no input into its design.

Fourthly, the majority of incidences of sexual harassment are
relatively minor and are a result of nothing more than bad man-
ners. As such they can be dealt with at the source. The ESB
pointed out that most complaints relate to the use of improper
language and to a lesser extent unwanted touching or feeling.[11]
Central to minimising such behaviour is the engendering of a cul-

---

[11] IBEC also quote research from the UK which found that "the most common form of sexual harassment is verbal, e.g. comments about clothing,
looks etc.". See IBEC, *The Law on Sexual Harassment*, undated pamphlet,
page 1.

ture that is harassment-free and not overreacting to the issue in the first place. As Clare Carroll of IBEC puts it:

> . . . the ultimate aim of a sexual harassment policy is to have sexual harassment regarded by all in the workplace as just another facet of misconduct which the employer will not tolerate. Sexual harassment, in even its more minor manifestations, is being treated as a hanging offence. Where we need to get to, is an acceptance by all concerned that, as most employees would accept, you don't come to work under the influence of alcohol or drugs, you don't have a punch-up with your fellow employees on the premises, you don't pilfer from your employer or your fellow-employees and you don't sexually harass your fellow employees.[12]

WHAT A SEXUAL HARASSMENT POLICY SHOULD CONTAIN

The policy should contain, at a minimum, the following broad pieces of information:

- A definition of sexual harassment;

- A strongly worded statement condemning sexual harassment;

- A description of the procedures to follow in submitting a claim;

- A statement regarding the obligations of all employees in dealing with sexual harassment;

- A list of the penalties for employees who breach this rule.

A Definition of Sexual Harassment

As has already been pointed out,[13] sexual harassment is best defined as discriminatory behaviour which is sexual in nature as well as unwelcomed and unreciprocated by the victim. Most un-

---

[12] Clare Carroll, "Employer Strategies and Initiatives", in a paper delivered to a conference entitled *Sexual Harassment in the Workplace, op. cit.*

[13] *Cf.* Chapter 1.

ion-management policies, however, tend to contain examples of sexual harassment. For example, IBEC's definition is:

> . . . conduct towards another person which is sexual in nature or which has a sexual dimension and is unwelcome to the recipient. Examples of harassment can include:

> *Verbal*

> • requests or demands for sexual favours

> • suggestive remarks

> • degrading abuse or insults

> • jokes or tricks of a sexual nature

> *Physical*

> • gesturing of a sexual nature

> • unnecessary touching

> • indecent exposure

> • actual assault, up to rape

> *Visual*

> • displaying pornographic material at the workplace.

> Sexual harassment should not be confused with simple friendly behaviour or with more intimate exchanges, if these are mutually desired and accepted.[14]

Making sure that employees know exactly what sexual harassment is can be helped by the inclusion of examples in a definition. Moreover, as Rubenstein has commented:

> Employers and trade unions may wish to consider whether a definition of sexual harassment in a policy statement or collective agreements should be supplemented by a list of examples, so as to make unequivocally clear what behaviours may be covered.

---

[14] IBEC, Guideline 4, *Dealing with Sexual Harassment in the Workplace*, (Dublin: IBEC, 1990), 1.

However, it must be emphasised that this list of behaviours should be regarded as illustrative rather than exhaustive.[15]

A Statement on Sexual Harassment

Organisations are legally obliged to take strong stands on sexual harassment. Central to this stand is a clear statement condemning sexual harassment and re-affirming the right of all staff, male and female, to a harassment-free environment. The ESB, as we have stated, has one, as does the Bank of Ireland. Dublin Bus, as another example, includes the following statement in its policy document on sexual harassment:

> Discrimination, direct or indirect, on the grounds of sex and/or marital status, in employment, in relation to pay and conditions of work will not be tolerated by the Company. Direct discrimination may be defined as less favourable treatment for people which is explicitly related to their sex and/or marital status. Indirect discrimination may be defined as an inessential requirement applied equally to both sexes or to married and single people of the same sex, but which has a disproportionate adverse effect on one sex or marital status.[16]

It is imperative that a culture that is supportive of this basic right to a harassment-free environment develops. IBEC has correctly pointed out that:

> If a sexual harassment policy is to work, it is important that it pervades the entire establishment and should not be confined only to the employer-employee or employee-employee relationships.[17]

Therefore, in designing a policy, an organisation has to consider those who will be affected by it. This may mean more than employees. Customers and suppliers may be affected, and in the case

---

[15] Michael Rubenstein, "What is Sexual Harassment?" (1992) 4 *Irish Industrial Relations Review*, Vol. 1, 7.

[16] Dublin Bus company policy, *Equal Opportunities: Sexual Harassment*, 1992, 2.

[17] *Sexual Harassment in Third-Level Institutions: Procedural Aspects.* (Dublin: IBEC, undated), 3.

of educational institutions, students must also be considered. As noted, the ESB is examining how to protect its employees in its shops from harassment by customers. All the major universities in Ireland, North and South, have policies on sexual harassment that address both students and staff, academic and non-academic. Queen's University in Belfast, for example, has an elaborate policy on sexual harassment. Not only does the university provide detailed guidelines to counsellors for handling complaints, but it also has special forms to complete when complaints are made. Educational institutions have a particular concern with sexual harassment because of the added dimension of student-staff relations.[18]

To summarise, a policy has to contain a statement, sufficiently worded, condemning sexual harassment. It is similar to a statement on total quality management (TQM). Quality has to involve *all* employees, and the policy has to be set at the very highest level of the firm. It is no different with a sexual harassment policy.

A company may wish to include two extra affirmations of rights in their policy. The first concerns the complainant. A policy may make it known that all employees have a right to complain, and that in making a complaint employees will not be victimised. The second statement concerns the rights of the person accused. These include, among other things, the right to a fair and impartial hearing and to a speedy resolution of the issue. IBEC advises employers to include a statement to the effect that false and malicious claims made by an employee will be subject to further disciplinary action. Some trade unionists claim that such a statement would deter employees from making complaints. The *Code of Practice* offers little help on this issue. It simply states that:

> It should be noted that where a complaint is not upheld by the formal investigation, this does not necessarily indicate that the

---

[18] At the time of going to press, University College Dublin (UCD) was being taken to the Labour Court by the UCD Students' Union over allegedly sexist posters which were displayed on campus. The case will be the first to have been taken under Section 6 of the Employment Equality Act which deals with discrimination in "learning environments". See "Union Joins UCD Sex Bias Case", *Irish Times*, 2 May 1995.

complaint was malicious. While a malicious complaint will generally be treated as misconduct under the disciplinary procedure, the application of this provision should not be such as to deter employees from bringing forward legitimate complaints.[19]

Procedures for Dealing with Sexual Harassment

An organisation has an obligation to assist the individual in making the initial step in filing a sexual harassment complaint. One way of doing this is to outline very clearly in a policy document the procedures that staff can and should take to make complaints. Employees should be encouraged to complain to the harasser first. The *Code of Practice* advises such an approach:

> Employees should be advised to attempt to resolve the problem informally if this is possible. The objective of an informal approach is to resolve the difficulty with the minimum of conflict. Employees should be advised to explain clearly to the perpetrator that the behaviour in question is unwelcome and offensive; it may be the case that the perpetrator does not realise the effect of the behaviour on the complainant. [20]

If a complainant is not successful in talking to the harasser, or alternatively, if she is uncomfortable with or unwilling to take such an approach, a complaint can be made to management. That requires the company having a clearly communicated and understood procedure for supervisors and managers. In its guidelines, the ESB provides the following advice for managers and supervisors:

> When a person comes to you wishing to lodge a grievance or complaint of sexual harassment, start by assuring them that you take the complaint seriously and that action will be taken quickly and discreetly. Be aware of the difficulties for the complainant i.e. embarrassment, fear of the outcome, etc. Ascertain

---

[19] *Op. Cit.*

[20] IBEC offers similar advice in its guidelines to employers. "An employee who is being sexually harassed should be encouraged, in the first place, to try to deal with it informally with the harasser, by stating that the behaviour is not welcome. If this does not succeed, the complaint should, normally, be processed through the grievance procedure". IBEC, *op. cit.*, 3.

the facts, express no opinion and make no commitment. Put aside your personal biases and allow the person to speak candidly. Encourage the complainant to clarify precisely what happened. [21]

Recognising the very obvious difficulty that some employees would have in making a complaint, the *Code of Practice* recommends that firms allow third parties to accompany an individual in making a complaint. A union representative could well be that third party. Companies are often advised to modify the grievance procedure in order to allow a complaint, for obvious reasons, to be made to a female member of staff. This staff member can in fact be a designated person. More likely it will be a senior manager whom the individual trusts. Existing grievance procedures typically make an employee's supervisor the first person to whom to make a complaint. Given the sensitive nature of sexual harassment, employees may be reluctant to discuss the issue with their supervisors. As such, the complainant should be given the option of complaining to someone she trusts.

Penalties

It is open to debate whether a sexual harassment policy should or should not outline, in specific or general terms, the penalties for anyone found to have breached company policy on sexual harassment. Some firms include them, others make no mention of them, while the majority make reference to existing disciplinary procedures. The latter are usually adequate for dealing with sexual harassment complaints.[22] Regardless of which option a firm takes, the main consideration is that there are penalties, that they are in line with the nature of the transgression, and that they are fairly and consistently implemented.

Regardless of whether staff, either directly or through their representatives, were involved in drawing up a policy, some employees, likely to be in the minority, will resent the imposition of

---

[21] ESB, *Guidelines for Managers and Supervisors, op. cit.,* 2.

[22] Clare Carroll of IBEC argues that: "Where discipline is involved, the employer must act in a consistent manner. Accordingly, there should be no special disciplinary procedure for sexual harassment". Carroll, *op. cit.*

penalties associated with sexual harassment. Despite these objections, as stated, an employer has an important obligation to all staff, and especially those whose vulnerability, for whatever reason, leaves them open to abuse. Sexual harassment policies are here to stay, and unless they are accompanied by some form of penalty, they are unlikely to be effective. Penalties should range from a verbal warning to dismissal. Nobody wishes to see a worker lose his (or her) job, but sexually harassing another worker is a serious offence and must be dealt with accordingly. Finally, Rubenstein[23] recommends including a clause stating that perpetrators are personally liable for committing acts of sexual harassment.

The issue of penalties is examined more thoroughly in the next chapter which deals with conducting sexual harassment investigations. As will be argued there, dismissal should only be used as a penalty when a thorough and fair investigation has been conducted.

HOW A POLICY SHOULD BE DRAWN UP

There are a number of ways in which an organisation can draw up a policy, ranging from designing one from scratch at one extreme, to availing of a policy supplied by IBEC or the EEA at the other. Most firms tend to use existing policies and add modifications as necessary.

Internally, an organisation should solicit support from staff. In unionised firms, a union (or unions as the case may be) may have to be consulted and agreement sought before a policy can become part of an industrial relations agreement. As will be pointed out in Chapter Six, while late to endorse women's rights, trade unions, especially those in the public sector, have made great strides in recent years in the area of employment equality. Having a union involved in drawing up a policy not only assists in the design of that policy, but also is likely to ensure greater acceptance of it by employees.[24]

---

[23] Rubenstein, *op. cit.*, 20.

[24] It is somewhat regrettable that the code, despite being the result of negotiations between the social partners, does not place an obligation upon em-

Once formulated, a sexual harassment policy should be communicated to all staff. One way of doing this is to include the policy in an employee handout. Unfortunately, an inherent disadvantage of this method is that sexual harassment policies get put in employee handbooks, usually towards the back, thus getting buried in the avalanche of information given to new employees. Further, the seriousness and complexity of the issue fails to get across. As IBEC, in addressing itself to employers, has argued:

> It is important to make it very clear to your employees that sexual harassment is a disciplinary offence. Too often, some employees and management staff as well think of sexual harassment as a bit of harmless fun. If that has been the attitude in your organisation, a specific statement to the effect that sexual harassment will be dealt with as part of your disciplinary procedure needs to be made. Different people have strikingly different ideas about what constitutes sexual harassment. It is vital that you, as an employer, make it quite plain to employees (and others, if necessary) what is considered in your organisation to be sexual harassment. [25]

For these reasons, firms should send memos to all employees outlining their sexual harassment policies. As Rubenstein advises, where sexual harassment policies form part of an overall employment equality policy, employers should make it a point to bring the section in the policy dealing with sexual harassment to the attention of employees. [26]

In addition to memos, the policy should be posted in suitable places. Employees rarely object to this, as most of them recognise

---

ployers to negotiate sexual harassment policies with unions. Despite acknowledging sexual harassment as "an issue for trades unions, both as employers and employee representatives" (page 18) and then elaborating on the role of unions in this, the code simply states that "(t)he development of policies on sexual harassment *may be* carried out in consultation with employees or their representatives, as appropriate" (emphasis added). Rubenstein consistently refers to the importance of having union involvement in the design, communication and implementation of sexual harassment policies. The EEA maintains a similar view.

[25] IBEC, *Sexual Harassment in Third-Level Institutions: Procedural Aspects.* (Dublin: IBEC, undated), 1.

[26] Rubenstein, *op. cit.*, 19.

the need for clear and effective communication on sexual harassment.

Finally, management may wish to consider the use of staff meetings to make known the company's concern about sexual harassment. It should be remembered that the Labour Court has ruled that it is not enough to inform just management and supervisory staff of company guidelines, but all employees must be informed.[27] Staff meetings are the responsibility of first line management who should be encouraged to talk to the employees under their supervision about sexual harassment. An employer should also ensure that the policy on sexual harassment is consistently enforced throughout the whole organisation.

OTHER STRATEGIES

Making First Line Management Accountable

As part of first line management, supervisors are the direct link between managers and employees. They interact on a daily basis with employees, many of whom they know personally. They are responsible for the performance of the work group under their supervision. Part of this responsibility entails ensuring a work environment that is conducive to high productivity. One should, however, also note that:

> Paradoxically, the non-co-operation of line management and particularly supervisors can wreck the implementation of a sexual harassment policy. Their non-co-operation will ensure that implementation of a sexual harassment policy is, at best, patchy and inconsistent and, at worst, totally ineffective. [28]

For that reason, supervisors should be given appropriate training and support of top-level management. As stated earlier, in principle a policy document on sexual harassment originates at the highest level in the firm, but all employees, including their representatives, should be involved in the design of the document. It is clearly important that senior management endorse the document,

---

[27] DEE 1092.

[28] Carroll, *op. cit.,* 5 .

but the success of the policy, as with TQM, will largely depend on supervisors and managers. They have to educate their employees, and they have to ensure compliance with company policy. They may also have to respond to complaints.

The need for training must be highlighted. Many supervisors and managers will themselves be unaware of what sexual harassment is (though some, of course will have experienced it). Worse still, they will be afraid of being asked to deal with complaints that may end up in the Labour Court. To make them responsible for policing a policy, as the ESB has done, they need extra training, and they need to know that they have the support and encouragement of senior management. The drawing up of appropriate guidelines is equally important.

Supervisors understandably can be apprehensive about being given a policing role on sexual harassment. They may also see dealing with sexual harassment as being the responsibility of the personnel department. The organisation therefore needs to convey to all supervisors that it is part of their duties, and that it is something which supervisors can, and indeed are expected, to handle.

Information remains at the heart of an effective sexual harassment policy. Supervisors cannot be expected to play a pivotal role unless they know what to do when someone makes a complaint. Some supervisors may feel that they are incapable of handling sexual harassment complaints because they lack the necessary skills. Organisations need to reassure supervisors that handling the initial complaints of sexual harassment is a task that they are well qualified to undertake.

At the very least, supervisors should be able to access advice, or, if necessary, refer complaints to a higher authority. Supervisors cannot afford to downplay the issue and ignore the complaint. That said, supervisors should not react by treating all initial complaints of sexual harassment as amounting to serious offences. Quite possibly, the imposition of a new sexual harassment policy will give rise to frivolous complaints. The supervisor has to be able to distinguish between such complaints and incidents where serious breaches of complaint have occurred. He or she will also need to know when to handle a complaint on his or her own and when to seek the advice of senior management. Again, training and the provision of guidelines are critical.

Training in the Area of Sexual Harassment

Some organisations may opt to send supervisors, including managers in supervisory positions, on training courses. Good as this idea sounds, few organisations offer training in this area, and training can be expensive. Aside from private management consultants, the largest organisation offering training in this field is the Dublin Rape Crisis Centre. The Employment Equality Agency provides free advice to companies, trade unions and individuals, but it does not itself provide training. An alternative suggestion is for an organisation to provide its own training. Making one person in the organisation, after appropriate training, responsible for overall policy, as well as the provision of information and guidelines, can make for sound policy. The designated person can then provide training, as well as support and advice, in the organisation.

At the very least, an internal training package should include full information on what the policy of the organisation is, and what the role of supervisors and managers in dealing with sexual harassment is. It is equally important to make supervisors and managers aware that not only does the organisation have a strong policy on sexual harassment, but that they have the support of the company in dealing with it. This type of training is best delivered in-house.

Another aspect of training concerns an awareness of people and how they interact with each other at the workplace. This is sometimes called interpersonal communication. Supervisors and managers need to understand how people operate, not necessarily as individuals, but certainly as members of groups. Generally speaking, when men or women work separately, sexual harassment is less likely to occur. In contrast, where one has mixed groups, the potential for sexual behaviour of a negative kind to occur is quite high. Employees have to be aware that sexual harassment is part of human nature, albeit a negative part. Sexual harassment training is difficult, though not impossible to get. Some people may be offended by the perspective this training offers — for example, most consultants in this field talk about raising consciousness about women, gender awareness, sensitivity training, etc. Regardless of personal objections, however, it is better to offend a small minority so that the majority of employees can work productively and peacefully.

Figure 4.1 shows IBEC's recommendations on policy statements dealing with sexual harassment

Figure 4.1: IBEC's Recommendation on Policy Statements Dealing with Sexual Harassment[29]

Management should first of all formulate a policy on sexual harassment. This policy should include:
- a statement of what is considered to be sexual harassment
- a statement of management's intention to treat sexual harassment as misconduct under the disciplinary procedure in force in the employment
- a requirement for staff suffering sexual harassment to report the matter to their immediate supervisor
- the provision of an alternative complaints route where reporting to the immediate supervisor would be inappropriate
- an undertaking to deal seriously and confidentially with allegations of sexual harassment.

This should be accompanied by appropriate training and advice for management and supervisory staff in order to:
- ensure consistent attitudes towards the problem
- ensure that complaints are dealt with through the grievance procedures to prevent the occurrence or reoccurrence of sexual harassment in the areas under their direct supervision or general control.

---

[29] IBEC, *op. cit.*, 2.

CHAPTER FIVE

CONDUCTING A SEXUAL HARASSMENT INVESTIGATION

Confronting the issue of harassment will minimise potential problems and . . . improve the overall harmony and smooth functioning of the workplace.[1]

INTRODUCTION

While a policy document clarifies the meaning of the term sexual harassment, explains what an employee should do if she is being sexually harassed and outlines the nature of complaints procedures and penalties, an employer does not fulfil his or her duties simply by implementing one. Rather, he or she must also be willing to conduct sexual harassment investigations and, if necessary, discipline harassers. This chapter outlines how a complaint of sexual harassment should be investigated.

In brief, the full procedure for handling a complaint is as follows:

1. Initiate an investigation immediately if a written complaint is lodged. When an oral complaint is made its gravity should be assessed before any decision is made. An investigation will, however, usually be required.

2. Gather as much information as possible from relevant sources. Interview the main parties and any witnesses. Document the entire process.

3. The investigator, alone or as part of an investigating committee, must make a judgement and take any required action.

---

[1] Carmel Foley, "Why We Need a Code of Practice", *Making Advances — A Conference on Sexual Harassment in the Workplace*, Dublin, 15 October 1993.

4. Follow-up on the investigation providing counselling for any victims and, if necessary, initiating disciplinary action.

Although, in principle, it is easy to outline what a sexual harassment investigation entails, few investigations have ever been conducted in Irish companies. That having been said, following the procedures and guidelines offered in this chapter should help an employer to conduct a fair and thorough investigation.

INVESTIGATING A COMPLAINT

Once an allegation of sexual harassment is made, no matter how trivial it may seem, an employer should conduct an investigation. Such an investigation should have one central aim: to determine, to the greatest extent possible, what actually occurred.

Even where there are no formal procedures in place, the investigator should ensure that he or she abides by the rules of natural justice. The investigation should be fair and impartial. Siding with the person making the accusations, or alternatively, dismissing their accusations out of hand, is not an impartial and fair investigation. The investigation should be initiated promptly and completed quickly, as well as being thorough. These goals are not incompatible. Once an allegation of sexual harassment is made, people expect to see results. They will also inevitably take sides, drawing their own conclusions. "I think she is right", or "he did not mean it that way" will be the likely comments of staff members. Therefore, an investigation should begin and conclude as quickly as possible.

For an investigation to be thorough, everyone involved should be interviewed, and in the same manner. In being thorough, however, the investigator should concentrate primarily on the factual issues involved. Sexual harassment is a very emotional issue, and this can often lead to distorted information, exaggeration and the like. Only information that is relevant to the issue at hand, and that is factual, should be collected. All records should be kept in a safe place and no unauthorised person should have access to them.

An Open or Closed Investigation?

The experience from America suggests that an open investigation is far better than a confidential or secretive one. To begin with, it means the issue can be addressed in specific terms, and the root of the problem addressed quickly. Indeed, it is almost impossible to conduct an investigation, and particularly interviews, without naming people. Secondly, people have a right to know who has made allegations about them. Finally, revealing the name of the person may prevent rumours spreading. It is better in many incidences to be open about an investigation since this way it avoids gossip.

The investigator has to decide whether or not to reveal the names of the people involved after careful analysis of the facts. This must take account of company policy as well the reputations and feelings of the individuals involved. However, if the investigator decides to reveal one name, then all names should be revealed. If, on the other hand, the investigator chooses not to reveal names, he or she should use objective language such as "a staff member or members alleged that another staff member. . . ." Sexual harassment investigations in America seem to heading in the direction of minimal confidentiality. It is suggested that the Irish process should follow likewise.

Who Should Conduct Sexual Harassment Investigations?

A sexual harassment investigation is a serious, if infrequent, type of investigation. Those directly connected will be opinionated about the issue; those on the periphery, naturally curious. Also, the organisation itself may be concerned about the legal ramifications, particularly its liability. Who then should conduct the sexual harassment investigations?

There are no experts, no qualifications, at least on paper, which make one person skilled at conducting sexual harassment investigations, and another not. Rather, an investigator should be familiar with company policy on sexual harassment, as well as the law on the area. Ideally, the person should be capable of conducting a legal investigation, preferably having experience in dealing with employee grievances and the like. That does not necessarily mean a lawyer, but rather someone who is familiar with legal principles and procedures. They should be sympathetic to the problem, but not biased one way or the other.

Some organisations might feel that a woman is preferable. This need not be the case. The best individual, male or female, is one who is professional and competent. Any manager with the right interpersonal skills can do it. However, the manager must be senior to those who are being investigated and must act with the support and full knowledge of senior management. This individual may need training both in legal procedures and in the area of sexual harassment itself. Finally, the individual may need support in conducting investigations, such as secretarial assistance in the typing and collating of information or legal advice.

The norm in most large organisations is to designate one or more persons who are responsible for conducting sexual harassment investigations. Large organisations usually have an equality officer, that is, someone who is responsible for the entire policy on employment equality. In small to medium-sized firms, it is not possible to designate someone with this authority. Instead, a senior employee or head of the firm should conduct the investigation. Naturally, such an individual should not be directly involved in the incident which led to the allegation.

A Plan of Action: The First Step in the Investigation

Even before the investigation begins, the investigator has to plan a course of action and prepare a list of people to interview along with a list of questions that can be used in the interviews. In addition, a time schedule needs to be set in place. Finally, as mentioned, the investigator should become familiar with all the facts pertaining to sexual harassment, particularly the law and company policy. If unsure of the procedures and practices, the investigator should consult outside help. One source of advice, for member companies, is IBEC. Alternatively, the Employment Equality Agency provides free advice.

STARTING THE INTERVIEWS

Interviewees fall into two categories: those directly involved (the complainant and the person accused) and those on the periphery (witnesses). Supervisors, fellow employees and managers all tend to make reliable witnesses. Interviewing witnesses allows the investigator to collaborate and to establish beyond reasonable doubt the facts of the case.

Typically, the most important people to interview are those directly connected with the issue; they should be interviewed first. That way the investigator can get to the heart of the problem quickly and discount any frivolous claims before they get out of hand. Rather like mediation in an industrial relations dispute, a settlement can be reached quickly with minimum disruption. However, a sexual harassment complaint is unlike any normal grievance. The issue is very emotional, with typically no easy settlement available, and attempting to downplay the issue can in time undermine morale and trust in a firm. Therefore, once a sexual harassment investigation has begun it should be carried through to the end so that *all* relevant persons are interviewed.

If the complaint is being referred to an investigator by a third party, it might be best to speak first with the complainant's supervisor or manager or whoever made the referral. Managers tend to be more objective and will help in getting to the facts. Similarly, when there are many allegations of sexual harassment, the investigator may choose to begin with witnesses. Where there is a very specific allegation of sexual harassment occurs, it is best usually to begin with the complainant herself.

CONDUCTING THE INTERVIEW

What follows next is an analysis of three types of interviews: with the complainant, with the person accused, and with witnesses. In effect, all three sets of interviews follow the same rules.[2] The interviewee should ideally sit opposite the interviewer, and all interviews should be held in a private office, out of the way of other employees. While it is important at all times to make the person feel at ease, the interviewee should be informed as to the purpose of the meeting and why they are being interviewed. It is important to ensure that the interviewee understands the exact purpose of the interview. Further, each interviewee should be asked

---

[2] For further information on how to conduct interviews, see Noel Harvey, "Effective Supervisory Management in Ireland" (Dublin: NCIR Press, 1994), Chapter Seven.

not to discuss details of their interview with other people and should be told when and how they will be informed as to the outcome of the investigation.

Like the disciplinary interview, the sexual harassment interview is a semi-structured one. That is, the investigator asks questions from a prepared questionnaire, but strays from the questionnaire when the occasion demands.

The investigator should keep good notes. While taking notes, however, the investigator should look for signs in the way a person acts that can indicate a person's beliefs and feelings. A person who feels strongly about the issue will be likely to show that. These cues can be helpful in making sense of conflicting information. As the interviews proceed, the investigator will get a sense of the seriousness of the allegation(s) made.

Some organisations prefer to use at least two people for interviewing, with at least one male and one female interviewer. There are good reasons for doing this. A panel of interviewers are generally more adept at getting at the facts of the case than one person. Plus, while one individual can ask questions, the other can take notes, often alternating roles. Finally, two or more people can offer a wider view of the issue. One of these may be a specialist in personnel management or law which adds much to the quality of the interview. However, having one person conduct the interview allows for greater confidentiality, as well as helping to relax the interviewee. Two or people conducting the interview could be interpreted by an interviewee as threatening. The number of people who sit in on the interview board, therefore, should be decided by the organisation. The analysis that follows deals with one person interviews.

Meeting with the Complainant

The complainant needs to be reassured that she was right to make a complaint and that the organisation will take it seriously. Mention should be made also that, as part of the procedure, the person accused will have to be interviewed and that his rights, too, have to be safeguarded. Once the complainant understands this, the investigator should explain fully the process involved, and without prejudicing themselves or the organisation, the possible outcomes.

It is a good idea for the investigator to ask a few questions to get the interview off the ground and to ensure that the facts at the disposal of the interviewer are indeed correct. This helps to get the talk flowing. Early on in the interview the investigator should ask the complainant to explain, in her own words, what exactly happened. The investigator should let the individual do the bulk of the talking, only prompting her to make sure the interview stays on track. At no stage should the investigator interfere to the point of steering the interview in a particular direction, nor should he or she make any judgement at this stage.

Sample Questions for the Complainant

The following is a list of questions that can be used in an interview with the complainant. These are suggested questions only, which should be adjusted to suit a particular organisation and/or situation.

- Tell me, in your own words, what happened? Take your time.

- When did the incident occur?

- Was there anyone else present?

- Did you tell anyone else about the incident(s)?

- Have you any documentary evidence about the incident(s)?

- What is the name of the person you say harassed you? Did you know him before the incident?

- How much contact do you have with him in work?

- Have you any contact with him outside of work?

- Where did it happen? Was it in the workplace?

- What did he say to you? Try to remember his exact words.

- What happened immediately after the incident? Did he say anything? Did he threaten you?

- Did he treat the incident as a joke, or was he serious? What was your impression of him at the time of incident?

- Have you ever objected to this man before?

- Was it a sudden and unexpected incident? Had you any idea that this was going to happen?

- In your view, has anyone else in the department/office been harassed? By this man or others?

- What are your relations like in your department/office now?

- What is your relationship with this individual now?

- Does your manager/supervisor know about the incident(s)? Do you have a good working relationship with your supervisor and/or manager?

- Do you understand the seriousness of the accusations you are making?

- What do you expect to happen now? If given the option, what would you like to see happen? Do you think you can still work with this individual now?

Questions that Should Not be Asked

The investigator should avoid judgmental or sexist questions such as:

- Have you no sense of humour?

- Do you not like a bit of fun around the office?

- Did you lead him on?

- What were you wearing? What do you expect with a dress like that?

- Why didn't you complain before?

- Are you a feminist?

- [Name] is a nice fellow. Are you sure you did not misunderstand him?

- Have you ever slept with him? Do you sleep with others? Are you sexually promiscuous?

- Have you ever before made an allegation of sexual harassment? Why not?

Concluding the Interview

Before concluding the interview the investigator should have the complainant record her complaint in writing. This is not always possible since she may be very emotional. If that is the case, a written record can be made later. The investigator should make a full report of the interview, however. That report should be begun immediately while his or her memory is fresh. It is equally important to record any questions that need to be followed up, and to revise, if necessary, any other prepared questionnaires. No judgement should be made as yet.

Meeting with the Accused

Once the complainant has been interviewed, and the document and testimony examined, the investigator should prepare to interview the accused. He should be informed well in advance of the meeting and that he is legally entitled to legal or union representation.

As before, the interview should be conducted in a private office and begun by making the person accused aware of the purpose of the meeting.

Having explained the purpose of the meeting, the investigator should present full details of the allegations made. These should be presented clearly and without interruption or emotion. It is quite possible that the investigator will have to disclose the identity of the complainant. The investigator should study the reactions of the accused. As noted, body language is often a good indicator of what a person is thinking.

The accused should then be asked to explain in his own words his account of the incident/incidents. There should be no interruptions. Instead, the investigator should listen carefully and take notes. However, the investigator should aim to get a complete account of the alleged incident(s). This may necessitate some involvement on the part of investigator to ensure that the facts are ascertained.

The typical defence of a person accused is one of the following:

- The first defence made is often denial. (It never happened).

- The second is to claim it was only fun, that no harm was done, and that the victim participated and welcomed it.

- The third is to say that nobody had complained before and that the individual was not told it was wrong.

Individuals rarely admit to having harassed co-workers. Regardless of what the accused says, the first responsibility of the investigator is to conduct an impartial review. In so doing, the investigator should not only resist making an early judgement but also decline from getting involved in any way. This means not siding with the individual or attempting to entrap him. Rather, it means asking the right questions, and recording the answers.

The interview with the accused has the potential, perhaps more than any other interview, to get heated. The accused may react strongly claiming victimisation or an abuse of his rights. If this is the case, the investigator has to choose a course of action. Typically the first is to calm the individual down, explaining to him that this is a preliminary interview designed to obtain facts. If this is not successful, it may be necessary to adjourn the interview until the person has calmed down.

What happens if the individual becomes abusive and threatens or questions the authority of the investigator? This is where good preparation comes into play. The investigator has to be aware of company and legal policy and his authority insofar as the investigation goes. Therefore, if the accused questions the investigator's authority, it must be pointed out very clearly that he or she is acting in the proper manner as defined by company policy. If the meeting becomes more heated still, it may be necessary to postpone it. The investigator should not become embroiled in a personal exchange and should continue to act in a professional manner. If a further meeting ends in a similar situation, the allegations can then be made in writing.

Sample Questions for the Person Accused

- Do you know what sexual harassment is? Are you aware of company policy on sexual harassment?

- Are your aware of the complaint made against you by a member of the staff?

- What is your response to this complaint?

- Did the alleged incident(s) take place?

- Tell me, in your own words, what exactly happened?

- What is your job in the organisation?

- How long have you worked in the organisation? How long in this particular department/office?

- How well do you know this person?

- What is your relationship with the individual?

- Do you know this person outside of work?

- What exactly did you say to her?

- What did she say to you?

- Did you physically touch her in any way?

- What was her reaction?

- Did she complain or resist in any way?

- Were there any witnesses? Who are they? What did they see? Can they collaborate what you say?

- Are you on good terms with her? How long have you known her? Do you know this person outside of work?

- Have you ever behaved in a similar way with the person before this particular incident? If so, did she complain to you about it then?

- Have you ever had complaints like this about your alleged behaviour before? Why did you think she has made a complaint? How would you describe your fellow employees' opinion of yourself?

- What do you think is the best way to resolve this situation? What way would you like to see it resolved?

As with the interview with the complainant, leading questions should be avoided. Instead, questions should be specific and responses recorded. No judgement should be made.

Concluding the Interview

Unless, for whatever reason, either the investigator or the person accused terminates the meeting abruptly, the meeting should conclude on a positive note. In particular, the investigator should reiterate that this is a sexual harassment investigation, at its preliminary stage, and that, as yet, these are only allegations. It should be pointed out to the individual that the company will take it very seriously if he attempts in any manner to intimidate or threaten the person making the accusations. The accused should be advised that it is in his best interest to remain quiet about the issue, discussing it with either his legal or union representative but not fellow employees. Finally, assure the individual that the investigation will be conducted in a prompt and appropriate manner and that he will hear back from the investigator once the investigation is concluded.

Concluding the Investigation at this Point

As was pointed out earlier, very often one or two meetings are sufficient. That is, once having explained to the individual in question any possible transgression, assuming there is one, it is quite possible that this is sufficient. Many employees are willing to correct their behaviour once it is explained to them that it is wrong. Therefore, the investigation may be terminated at this point on the assurance that the harasser will not continue his behaviour.

There is nothing wrong with this action, though obviously there are some pitfalls. Because a person says he will cease a particular behaviour does not necessarily mean he will do so. Alternatively, a person can simply substitute one type of harassment for another. For example, if a male employee was accused of harassing a particular female employee by continuously asking her for a date, he could cease to ask for dates, but instead, as a form of retaliation, spread rumours about the individual in question. In the end, the matter is made worse.

Thus, the investigator has to make a judgement, based on the facts of the situation, as to the proper course of action. No matter what action, if any, is taken, a sexual harassment investigation does not end with interviews. Rather, as noted, the situation has to be monitored carefully, and often systems or procedures have to be put in place to ensure that a particular type of behaviour, if deemed offensive and contrary to company and legal policy, does not happen again. Or if it does, that action can be taken quickly and effectively.

The remainder of this chapter will deal with the question of taking a sexual harassment investigation further. Later, incidences where no complaint is made, and where the person who has alleged harassment has left the company, will be examined.

Meetings with Witnesses

Identifying witnesses is not a difficult task. People with some proximity to the individuals in question — a fellow worker, a supervisor or a manager — usually make good witnesses. However, the closer one individual is to the main parties, the more biased he or she is likely to be. By interviewing a range of people, however, the investigator is more likely to establish the true facts of what has happened.

The interviews with witnesses should begin with an account of why the interview is being conducted: it is a sexual harassment investigation designed to establish facts about a particular incident or incidents. The individual in question is not under investigation, but does have an obligation to assist. They have a right to union or legal representation.

The investigator should ask the individual his or her view or understanding of the situation. The individual should be asked to verify what has been said. Did he or she witness any incident? Did anyone confide in him or her? What, in the opinion of the witness, is the relationship between the complainant and the person accused?

The concern is not just with the gathering of facts, but also with assessing the credibility of the witness. Facts can be accumulated by asking a broad range of questions, taking note of the answers and double checking one person's account against another's. Credibility is a different matter. A person who has a close relationship with either of the individuals involved does not lean towards objectivity. On the other hand, they can be an excellent source of valuable information.

Witnesses' motivation is a good indicator of their credibility. Investigator should ask themselves why witnesses are making certain statements? Are they biased towards one person? What are their views on sexual harassment as a whole? Are they the sort of person who believes that the significance of sexual harassment is exaggerated? People who are extreme in their views are not always great witnesses. That is not to say that their testimony should be ignored, but it should be placed in its proper perspective. It is up to the investigator, based upon detailed consideration of the facts, to make the ultimate decision about a person's credibility.

Sample Questions for Witnesses
The following questions are based on the premise that the names are being revealed.

- Are you aware that an accusation of sexual harassment has been made?

- Do you know him? What is your relationship to him? Are you on good terms with him, for example? How long have you worked with him? Do you know him outside of work?

- Do you know her? What is your relationship to her? How long have you worked with her? Do you know her outside of work?

- How would you describe the atmosphere at work? Do people get along with each other? Are there any overall problems with relations between staff?

- Are you surprised that an allegation of sexual harassment was made? In your view, do you think that the allegation should or should not have been made? Is there any element of truth in it?

- What do you think really happened? Was this what you witnessed? If you were either party, what would you have done? Were there other witnesses, aside from yourself?

- Has the complainant ever talked to you about this? If so, what did you do?

- Has the accused ever talked to you about this or other incidents. What was your response or advise to him?

- Had the individuals in questions been romantically linked? Do they get well with each other? What do you think is going on?

- What sort of relationship do you have with the individuals now? What are relations like in the department as a whole?

Concluding the Meeting

The meeting should conclude in much the same way as it began, by reiterating the purpose of the meeting. The witness should be requested not to talk to anyone about the meeting and to maintain the same relationship as before with the main parties involved. The investigator should indicate that the investigation is still underway, and that the interviewee will be briefed, once it is concluded, on the outcome. The individuals should be thanked for their participation.

MAKING A JUDGEMENT

When all necessary interviews have been conducted, and when all the facts, insofar as they are facts, have been gathered, the investigator has to make a judgement. Part of this process will involve making a report to senior management. It may or may not entail the investigator implementing disciplinary action, but a report has to be made. In that report, the investigator has to reach a decision, supported by the facts of the case, that an allegation either does or does not have truth in it.

Some investigations by their very nature will lend themselves to easy judgement. As noted earlier, a discussion with the main parties can often resolve the issue to the satisfaction of all concerned. In other cases, incidents of sexual harassment are so blatant that interviewing relevant others is hardly necessary. However, there are times when investigations give rise to very divergent accounts, and differences of opinions that make the job of reaching a decision very difficult. However, following a simple process can do much to help one reach the correct decision:

1. The investigator gathers all the information and brings it together in one form, namely the portfolio.

2. This portfolio is examined carefully.

3. Isolate what is factual and what is unsubstantiated hearsay. The latter should be ignored. Similarly, information that is subject to debate or has been denied should be isolated. The testimony and supporting information is read carefully in order to establish collaborated facts. Judgement should be avoided at this stage.

4. With the factual information at hand, start to piece together the information that will support a final decision. The investigator should look for very serious and very clear indicators of allegations or denials of sexual harassment.

5. The investigator should write down the judgement, supporting it at all times with the facts. If it cannot be supported, then it cannot stand as a judgement. In reaching a judgement the investigator should keep in mind the fact that it is not the intention of the harasser but the response of the victim that is important.

POST-INVESTIGATION ACTION

Once a judgement has been made, the investigator has to inform all parties of his or her conclusion and implement his or her recommendations. The latter may include post-investigation interviews, such as a counselling interview with the complainant and a disciplinary interview, if necessary, with the person accused. This section deals first with the complainant, partly because she, having made the initial complaint, should be the first to be informed of the outcome of the investigation.

Dealing with the Complainant

An individual who is harassed will suffer greatly. Stress, low self-esteem, and anger, are just some of the many symptoms experienced by victims of sexual harassment. A person who is harassed, and particularly where a serious incident of sexual harassment has occurred, may need counselling. So too may the harasser, especially an individual who feels himself wronged, or fails to understand the seriousness of the situation. Counselling interviews may be conducted by the investigator, by a senior manager, or in the case of serious incidents, by a trained counsellor.

Counselling may also be necessary where the complainant submits a weak or frivolous claim. An individual may submit a claim believing fully that she has been harassed, but the evidence may not support her beliefs. It is necessary to explain to the complainant why her claim was not upheld. While empathising with her, the investigator has to make organisational policy on sexual harassment clear to her and explain why her claim did not breach these rules. The investigator should make it known that this is perfectly natural, and will not in any sense prevent her from making future claims. If, in the judgement of the investigator, the complainant has not yet understood the reasons for her claim's rejection, then a follow-up interview, sometimes with a trained counsellor, may be necessary.

Perhaps the major criticism of the response to sexual harassment is that not only does the victim, who is usually a woman, suffer the indignation of the harassment and is rarely fully compensated for the distress she has suffered, but she often loses her job or is transferred as well. Many women leave jobs on account of harassment, but few harassers do. Companies make what is, in many cases, a prudent decision to transfer an individual who has experienced harassment. She may wish to establish a new beginning putting that chapter of her life associated with harassment behind her. The company should respect that wish, and do what can be done to fulfil it. However, she should not be forced to transfer to another office or department simply because she, quite rightly, refuses to work with the harasser. Again, the investigator has to make an informed judgement based on an understanding of the wishes of the people involved as to what is the best solution to the problem. If a transfer of the victim does occur, it should not be against her wishes and should be to a similar or better position. She should also be given the option, within a specified period if necessary, to return to her old job.

Dealing with the Person Accused

The person accused should be informed immediately after the complainant has been interviewed. In the event that the investigation has found no incident of sexual harassment, the person should be told that the investigation will not in any way prejudice his future with the company. The investigator will have to decide,

however, whether a permanent record should be added to the employee's personnel file.

If an investigation concludes that sexual harassment has occurred, then some form of disciplinary measures should be applied. Without the threat of discipline, employees will have far less respect for the policy and sexual harassment may be trivialised. However, disciplinary measures should be in line with the transgression and evenly applied to all staff. The firm's sexual harassment policy ideally should contain clear guidelines on what disciplinary measures are appropriate, and these measures should be communicated to all staff.

In disciplining a harasser, the investigator has to take into account the circumstances. These include the length and nature of the harassment, along with, perhaps, the views of the harasser and victim.[3] Minor breaches of company policy tend to be once-off incidents which are often regretted by the harasser and easily stopped. Serious breaches occur, not just in terms of the nature of the harassment, such as assault, but over time and when the harasser knew full well that his behaviour was harassing another and that was his intention. Serious breaches have to be dealt with using the full force of the company's disciplinary procedures. Disciplinary measures, which vary from organisation to organisation, include the following:

- written and/or verbal warning;

- denial/deferral of a raise and/or promotion;

- transfer;

- suspension;

- demotion;

- dismissal.

An organisation's disciplinary and grievance procedure should be adequate, with some modification, for dealing with sexual harassment issues. As Clare Carroll of IBEC points out, however,

---

[3] IBEC are adamant that the victim should have no input into the disciplinary process.

disciplinary procedures don't always encompass appropriate measures for dealing with sexual harassment:

> . . . the disciplinary codes may need small alterations. For example, many of them don't make specific provision for transfer and demotion as a possible disciplinary penalty. Disciplinary procedures should now make provision for such penalties, as they are likely to be needed from time to time by employers as a suitable response to a sexual harassment offence.[4]

The *primary* objective in implementing a disciplinary measure is not necessarily the harasser but, rather, to stop the harassment. However, there are times when strong disciplinary measures are necessary and have to be implemented, and be seen to be implemented. An organisation has to send a clear signal to staff that sexual harassment is wrong, and any transgressions of company policy will be dealt with accordingly. If a woman feels wronged having been exposed to continuous harassment over the years, there is little an organisation can do to undo the past. But it can take action to deal with the future: the harassment can stop, and other people should not be harassed.

In some cases, no disciplinary measures may be necessary. However, the harasser must understand very clearly that his behaviour is wrong and has to be stopped. In the event that the behaviour continues, then further disciplinary measures should be used.

Even if disciplinary measures are to be used, there is much to be said for minimal sanctions. A warning and a letter to that effect can be placed in a person's personnel file. As noted, this should be clearly communicated to the individual and confirmed with the harasser in writing or in interview.

When is dismissal a proper form of penalty? If the incident or incidents of sexual harassment are serious enough, say where an assault has taken place. Similarly, in incidents where the person knowingly harassed another, when that harassment has taken an extreme form and been persistent and continuous, and if the vic-

---

[4] Clare Carroll, "Employer Strategies And Initiatives", in a paper delivered to a conference entitled *Sexual Harassment in the Workplace - Making Advances*, 15 October 1993.

tim has suffered greatly as a result of harassment, the harasser should be dismissed from his job. Dismissal in this case should not just be seen as a punishment for what happened, but as a form of protection against the individual in question harassing another employee.

Some employees may argue that dismissal is too excessive a penalty for sexual harassment. In these days of long-term unemployment, a similar job, indeed any job, is hard to come by. His chances of getting another job are made worse by the fact that other employers are less likely to employ someone who has been sacked from a job, whatever the reasons. These are plausible arguments, but neither does justice to the reality of sexual harassment. If someone is harassed excessively or persistently she is likely to suffer greatly. The person who does the harassing, on the other hand, does not suffer. Furthermore, this is not a case of punishing for the sake of it. Rather, an employer has to send a clear message to all staff that sexual harassment is not acceptable and won't be tolerated, and that serious breaches will be dealt with in the manner required, by dismissal.

In making a dismissal, certain procedures, legal and organisational, have to be followed. The individual must be informed in writing, given proper notice and afforded every opportunity to defend himself. The reasons for the dismissal have to be well documented in case the harasser sues the organisation for unfair dismissal.

Communicating the Results to Witnesses

Employees who participated in the sexual harassment investigation should be informed as to the result, as should senior management. This information should be covered in a confidential memo which should be concise and should reiterate company policy on sexual harassment as well as asking that witnesses not to discuss the investigation with others.

The purpose of a sexual harassment investigation is not to penalise someone, but, rather, to correct inappropriate behaviour and to prevent it from recurring. For this reason alone it is worth communicating the results to all staff. The following rule should apply: if confidentiality was maintained during the investigation, then confidentiality should also be maintained in respect of the findings of that investigation. If, however, an open investigation was conducted, then the findings of the investigation should be communicated to all staff.

EXCEPTIONS TO THE RULE

Thus far this chapter has dealt with situations where the complainant and the accused both work for the same company. This is not always the case, however, and there are other possible scenarios.

Where No Complaint Has Been Made

As was argued earlier, a sexual harassment investigation can be conducted even where no complaint has been made. A good manager should pay close attention to what staff think and do. Cases of sexual harassment, either isolated or protracted, may come to light, either as a result of observation or through listening to what employees have to say. A good manager therefore should be cognisant of tell-tale signs of sexual harassment, especially where staff gossip about particular individuals. Incidences of sexual harassment, especially those of a serious nature, will usually eventually come to the attention of management.

Another method for uncovering sexual harassment is interviewing, at least informally, employees who leave the job. Termed exit interviews, these are widely conducted in American firms. A person who is leaving a firm because of sexual harassment will usually have no qualms about disclosing the reason for her departure. Appraisal interviews are another way of determining what employees feel about their working environment. If an employee feels particularly strongly about an issue, he or she will concede it without much prompting.

Where People Are No Longer Employed or Not Employed

Sexual harassment cases do not always involve people who still work for the same company. A person may, for example, have been harassed and opted to leave a firm, seeing this as the only or best way of ending the harassment. After leaving, she may seek redress by taking an action for constructive dismissal before the Employment Appeals Tribunal.

In the event of a claim of constructive dismissal on the grounds of sexual harassment being made, a company should begin an investigation. Such investigations are, however, difficult to undertake. Without the opportunity to interview the individual who has made the claim, the company is put in the difficult position of fighting a case before the Employment Appeals Tribunal while simultaneously attempting to get at the facts of the case.

Another scenario is where non-employees harass employees. For example, a delivery person may direct lewd remarks at females in an office. The fact that someone does not work for a company does not in any sense diminish a company's moral responsibility towards its employees. The harasser and his employer should be informed that his behaviour is unacceptable and must be stopped. If a warning, as the first step, does not result in the desired action, then a manager may have to write to the person's employer with a formal complaint. That should resolve the matter.

More complicated are incidents where customers of firms are involved. Nobody likes to annoy customers, especially those who are held in high esteem by the firm. However, employers have to take into account their important obligation towards staff, which by far outweighs their obligations towards customers. An employer in such circumstances simply has to inform the customer of the problems his behaviour causes and ask him to stop.

SUMMARY

Conducting sexual harassment investigations is an infrequent activity, and also an unpleasant and unrewarding one, but it has to be done. Policies without some form of penalty are totally ineffective. And before penalties can be administered an investigation has to be conducted to discern the facts.

Sexual harassment investigations should be conducted in accordance with a number of basic principles: they must be fair, impartial, prompt, and thorough. They are generally conducted by senior management, sometimes alone and sometimes as a group. In carrying out the investigation, the investigator aims to establish what happened, and if what happened amounts to sexual harassment. Interviews are the primary means of gathering information. Aside from interviewing the main parties, witnesses are interviewed in order to collaborate and thus establish, beyond all reasonable doubt what happened.

From there a judgement is made which must be supported by the facts. This then has to be communicated to those interviewed and to senior management. The action that has to be taken after the investigation may need to go beyond discipline, if any, and communication. Rather, the company should be conscious of its obligation to staff by providing, if necessary, counselling for the complainant and the person accused.

Figure 5.1 summarises the main steps in conducting a sexual harassment investigation.

Figure 5.1: How to Conduct a Sexual Harassment Investigation

1. Study organisational policy and the law on sexual harassment.

2. Devise a plan, including a timetable, for carrying out the investigation.

3. Compile a questionnaire.

4. Be aware that the investigation must be timely, impartial, fair and thorough.

5. Interview the complainant, the person accused and relevant witnesses.

6. Document and then evaluate the information collected.

7. Make a judgement supported by the facts.

8. Take appropriate action.

9. Monitor and follow up.

CHAPTER SIX

TRADE UNIONS AND SEXUAL HARASSMENT

In my admittedly biased view, our unions have achieved much praiseworthy work in this field. After a slow and edgy start, the trade union movement gradually entered the frame by suggesting ways of combating the problem in the workplace, particularly as many of the harassers are members of the same union as the victims.[1]

Introduction

Trade unions have a primary and important role to play in relation to sexual harassment. That role extends far beyond providing representation for union members in Labour Court hearings. Rather, unions can make an important contribution to society by educating workers — member and non-member alike — about the nature and effect of sexual harassment. And unions can and should insist that employers adopt strong polices on sexual harassment. They should similarly help in formulating this policy as well as in communicating it to workers. And they should, most importantly, insist that employers and employees abide by the spirit and intent of the law. In all, there is much a union can do to limit incidences of sexual harassment in the workplace. And this is dependent less on the willingness of employers to involve unions, and more on the union taking a proactive role in leading the fight against sexual harassment.

Employer reluctance is no reason for inaction on the part of the union official. In fact, the ICTU has called on all member unions to ensure that employers have policies in place, and that unions educate all workers (not just women) about sexual harassment.

---

[1] Terry Pattinson, *Sexual Harassment: The Hidden* Facts (London: Futura, 1991), 115.

The EEA, in numerous publications, and notably in the Irish *Code of Practice* which they drafted, has stated that employers should negotiate policies with unions. There is also an abundance of information on how they should do it, from the ICTU and other union federations abroad. This chapter will draw much on material supplied from the ICTU, the TUC, the AFL-CIO[2] in America and from interviews with various Irish trade union officials.

Why Unions Should Be Concerned About Sexual Harassment

Trade unions have to be concerned about sexual harassment. Members who feel stressed, cheated and abused have a right to have that situation corrected. The fact that one member can allege harassment by another is a poor excuse for a union not taking action. Equally, if one member makes a complaint and the majority of the union membership is oblivious to the problem, the union should not hide behind the majority view. Indeed, by doing little or nothing to stop the problem, trade union officials are inadvertently adding to it. Further, they are not fulfilling an important legal and moral obligation, namely the duty to represent their members. Finally, sexual harassment is also a safety and health issue for trade unions. As the ICTU argues:

> [Sexual harassment] creates an unpleasant and intimidating work environment, threatens job security and undermines equality in the workplace. Unions must take steps to ensure a safe and healthy work environment for all workers. [3]

---

[2] The American Federation of Labor-Congress of Industrial Organisations is the trade union congress for American unions. It is, therefore, the American equivalent to the ICTU or the TUC. The AFL-CIO has produced a booklet on the issue; see AFL-CIO, "Sexual Harassment in the Workplace: A Practical Guide". (Washington, DC, 1993). Reference will also be made to "How the Union Rep Can Stop Sexual Harassment", an informational brochure produced by Labor Notes, Detroit, Michigan, undated.

[3] ICTU, "Guidelines on Sexual Harassment" (Dublin: ICTU, undated), 1.

UNIONS AND WOMEN

The image of a typical trade union member is one clothed in overalls, working with his hands more than his head, and male. A carpenter, a bus conductor, or a factory worker are your typical union workers. In many cases, these stereotypical images of union workers are true. The earliest trade unions were for skilled manual workers: carpenters, printers, and stonemasons were the first craft workers to form unions. All specifically excluded women. Employment opportunities did not open up for women until well into the 20th century, and even then it did so only for single women in certain occupations, such as secretarial work and nursing.

Since about the 1960s, however, trade unions began to spread among public sector workers. These public sector unions, among them IMPACT and MSF (as they are called now), attracted women in untold numbers. As women joined trade unions, "women issues" began to attract the attention of full-time union officials. Employment equality became the leading issue of the day. The demise of the marriage bar in the civil service and equal pay for women owe much to strong bargaining by trade unions, along with European pressure. Unions today continue to push issues which are favoured more by women: tax relief for child care, crèche provisions in firms, low pay, etc. Sexual harassment is perhaps the latest in a line of issues that unions are beginning to respond to as a result of pressure exerted from membership, particularly female members.

Women as Full-time Unions Officials

Despite many strides made by unions in the area of employment equality, unions themselves are no harbingers of social or sexual change. Few women occupy full-time union positions. Indeed, even in unions where women predominate as members, they are underrepresented in full-time positions. Figures released by the ICTU show that women are a long way behind men in terms of full-time executive positions. For example, in 1993 women made up 38 per cent of ICTU-affiliated union membership,[4] yet only six trade unions (out of 70 trade unions affiliated to ICTU) had women represented on their executive committee in proportion to or greater than their female membership. In one trade union, ironically INTO (Irish National Teachers Organisation) with 78 per cent female membership, only 13 per cent of its executive committee were female. The figures are no better for employees of trade unions. Of the 314 full time trade union officials in the Republic of Ireland, only 15 per cent were female. Finally, 29 per cent of full time officials at the ICTU were female. This figure drops to 17 per cent, or five members, for the executive council of the ICTU, and four of those five are reserved seats. The ICTU, along with its equivalent body in the UK, the TUC, has actively encouraged unions to hire women into full-time positions and to afford women equal access to trade union education. Thus far, few unions have reached the goals set by the ICTU's equality programme.

Women can make a valuable contribution to trade union organisation and be utilised in all positions in the union, from shop steward to full-time official. By hiring women as full-time officials, by not discriminating against women in filling positions within the unions and in training opportunities, by actively encouraging women to be shop stewards, and finally by pushing equality issues in the workplace unions can set the right example in society for employers and for workers.

UNIONS AND SEXUAL HARASSMENT: THE ROLE OF THE ICTU

The Irish Congress of Trade Unions (ICTU) has stated that sexual harassment is an infringement of worker rights and that unions can and will take action to assert that right. Since 1984 it has advised member unions to negotiate policies on sexual harassment and employment equality. Where there are policies in place, or when they have been put in place, the ICTU has further

---

[4] These figures are extracted from an ICTU report, *Mainstreaming Equality, 1993-98* (Dublin: ICTU, 1993). See also ICTU, *Report of the Executive Council, 1993-95* (Dublin: ICTU, 1995), 69-71.

advised member unions to avail of the avenues provided by these policies to make complaints rather than, say, using the Labour Court.

In order to encourage member unions to take a proactive stance, the ICTU provides an important educational role by filtering information on employment equality in general, and sexual harassment in particular, to member unions.[5] This information can then be disseminated to individual workers, either from unions or indeed direct from the ICTU. Finally, the ICTU has fulfilled an important political or legislative functions. They were successful in negotiating a clause within the current national agreement, the Programme for Competitiveness and Work (PCW), which called upon the EEA to devise, with the involvement of the social partners, a *Code of Practice* on employment equality. That code came into effect in 1994. The ICTU is currently requesting that many of the provisions of the *Code*, which impose a moral obligation on employers, be given the force of law, and were instrumental in including a clause in the PCW to that effect. Aside from giving force of law to the *Code of Practice*, the ICTU has recommended that the Department of Equality and Law Reform seek funding from the European Commission for an informational and training programme aimed at increasing awareness of sexual harassment among employers and workers.

In an interview with Margaret Nolan,[6] Training and Equality Officer with ICTU, she argued the fact that most large companies have policies is testimony to union pressure. Further, the fact that the majority of cases that go to the Labour Court involve

---

[5] ICTU publishes the following material which is available to member unions and individual trade unionists: *Positive Action for Equal Opportunities at Work: Guidelines for Negotiators; Guidelines on Sexual Harassment*. It also publishes *Women's Charter*, a policy document titled *Gay and Lesbian Rights in the Workplace: Guidelines for Negotiators*, and, finally, a policy document on Job Sharing.

[6] Nolan's views are also contained in a paper entitled "Trade Union Strategies and Initiatives for Dealing with Sexual Harassment", delivered to the EEA Conference on Sexual Harassment in the Workplace, 15 October 1993. That paper deals extensively with the ICTU's policy and recommendations on sexual harassment. It is available directly from the author at ICTU, Raglan Road, Dublin 4.

non-union firms is also proof that unions can process claims internally. This highlights the importance of having unions resolve issues of sexual harassment on the shopfloor. The Employment Equality Agency's view, reflected in the *Code of Practice*, is that allegations of sexual harassment, unless they are serious, should be handled at the source. Evidence from the ESB indicates that complaints themselves are made privately to management, particularly first-line management. However, trade unions do provide an informational role in making workers aware of sexual harassment, and can function as an encouragement to firms to implement policies.

Policies of Individual Unions

The union's role in combating sexual harassment begins with the publication of a policy document. Such documents can be used first, to educate what may be a reluctant if apathetic membership, and second, to encourage members, if they are being harassed, to make complaints. Trade unions further have to ensure that employers have policies on sexual harassment, and that members are willing and able to voice concern about the issue. The latter is dependent in part on training individual shop stewards and branch officials to handle complaints in a proper manner. But it depends most of all on imparting a culture within the union, from full-time official to ordinary member, that employment equality is a worthwhile and attainable goal.

Unions could do well to follow the approach of the Irish Bank Officials Association (IBOA), the main union for bank workers. They have produced a detailed leaflet on the subject.[7] Distributed free of charge to all members, the leaflet deals with:

- The meaning of the term "sexual harassment";

- Myths and misinformation about sexual harassment;

- The kinds of people who most at risk of becoming victims of sexual harassment;

- The consequences of sexual harassment;

---

[7] Irish Bank Officials Association: *Sexual Harassment Policy* (Dublin: IBOA, undated).

- Guidelines on dealing with sexual harassment;

- The role of the IBOA.

The 15-page brochure concludes with IBOA's policy with respect to the banks. The IBOA wants to see all banks have polices in place. In addition, the banks would implement procedures for handling complaints in a timely and sympathetic manner, including the provisions of counselling services for both victims and harassers. Currently only several leading banks — the AIB, the Bank of Ireland and Ulster Bank — have policies. The smaller banks are expected to follow suit. Despite being a first-class document, surprisingly, the booklet does not include a statement outlining the important role members can play in ensuring that harassment does not occur in the first place. It does however make it abundantly clear what the policy of the IBOA is:

> The goal of the IBOA is to make union members sensitive to the problem of sexual harassment and to create a culture which discourages sexual harassment and where harassment occurs, a climate where victims will feel comfortable turning to the union for assistance. [8]

SIPTU, Ireland's largest union with over 200,000 members, also has taken a strong stand on sexual harassment. Like the IBOA, they have distributed information on sexual harassment,[9] and raised member awareness of the issue by regular columns in their newsletter. The booklet is well presented, written in clear language and goes far in raising membership awareness of the issue. It includes a statement from the joint general presidents, as well as their Equality Officer, on sexual harassment. The booklet explains what sexual harassment is and the likely effects on a person who experiences harassment. The booklet also contains information on what shop stewards should do if they receive a complaint from a member. There is also a section outlining what

---

[8] IBOA, *op. cit.*, 11.

[9] SIPTU's brochure is titled "Sexual Harassment is No Joke!", and is published by the Equality Unit Services, Industrial and Professional Trade Union, Liberty Hall, Dublin 1.

should be in a policy document that would, ideally, be negotiated with the employer. SIPTU provides as extra material a sample policy as a guideline for negotiators in dealing with a particular company. Finally, as with the IBOA brochure, there is no express mention of members' obligation to maintaining a harassment-free environment. There is, however, a reference to the role of workers, in a section dealing with employers. It reads:

> Workers also have a role in ensuring that the work environment is free from sexual harassment. They too can contribute to preventing sexual harassment through an awareness and sensitivity towards the issue; and by ensuring that standards of conduct for themselves and for colleagues do not cause offence. They can discourage sexual harassment by making it clear that they find this behaviour unacceptable, and by supporting colleagues who are victims of such treatment and are considering making a complaint.[10]

SIPTU set up an internal woman's group that examine issues that relate to women. The ESBOA (ESB Officers Association), which has the largest female membership of all the ESB unions, jointly participates on a committee in the ESB which oversees policy on employment equality. The IBOA, similarly, has a committee to deal with women's affairs, and participates in numerous bank committees on employment equality. Finally, all three unions have equality officers, incidentally all female, who are responsible for day-to-day policy in the unions on employment equality.

Union Strategy on Sexual Harassment

No research has ever been conducted to ascertain what percentage of unions have sexual harassment policies. Informal estimates put the figure at about 70 per cent, most of which are unions with large female memberships.[11] Aside from the aforemen-

---

[10] SIPTU, *op cit.*, 14.

[11] This figure of 70 per cent came from ICTU and is purely an estimate. However, Margaret Nolan, Training and Equality Officer with ICTU, in a paper entitled "Trade Union Strategies and Initiatives for Dealing with Sexual Harassment", *op. cit.*, writes: "Since 1984 the vast majority of trade unions have developed policies on sexual harassment and are in the process of

tioned unions, these include all the teachers unions, the nurses unions, and the main public sector unions, including IMPACT, MSF, INO and the PSEU. The experiences of these unions, however, provide important lessons in the ways that sexual harassment policies can be improved.

The first and important lesson is the manner in which unions can forge discussion on the issue and raise member awareness. Borrowing from the TUC, the INO (Irish Nurses Organisation) in their policy document state:

> Sexual harassment is a serious work-place issue and as such is very much a trade union issue. The INO believe the more the question of sexual harassment is discussed openly in the workplace, the easier it will become to eliminate it.[12]

Trade unions can ensure greater discussion of the issue through the provision of material and training on sexual harassment. Despite a lot of talk about sexual harassment, many union members, especially male members, trivialise the issue. Some of these people, likely in the minority, may themselves be harassers. More likely, they are people for whom telling (and listening to) lewd jokes, making sexually explicit comments and gestures are all part of the daily routine of work. More to the point, these type of people are likely to form the bulk of union membership. This makes it especially difficult, though not impossible, for a union official to attempt to convince membership to take the issue seriously.

Trade unions should also augment organisational structures which are more adept at dealing with sexual harassment complaints. In the first instance, no differently from an employer, every trade union should have a designated official at branch level whose responsibility it is to provide advice and assistance to members. It is not necessary that the designated individual be female, but his or her name should be made known to all members in a union newsletter or leaflet on sexual harassment, and

---

providing training and information to their shop stewards and Branches". Page 2.

[12]Irish Nurses Organisation, "Sexual Harassment at Work: An Information Handbook for Members" (INO: Dublin), page 5.

members should be encouraged to avail of this service. Also, as SIPTU and other unions have done, a women's committee should be set up in the union to co-ordinate and manage all the union's activities with respect to employment equality.

The final aspect for trade unions concerns their relationship with employers. Unions should encourage employers to adopt policies on sexual harassment and employment equality. The ICTU, echoing what is in the *Code of Practice*, clearly opines that sexual harassment policies should be negotiated with the union. These in turn should form part of an equal opportunity document.[13] A negotiated approach represents an acknowledgement by an employer that a union has a role to play in preventing, or at least minimising, sexual harassment. The reality of industrial relations is very different, however. The ESB, as noted in Chapter Four, view sexual harassment as a managerial problem; the ESB group of unions, and notably the ESBOA, is informed about policy change but not necessarily consulted. Many of the leading banks have policies which were not negotiated with the IBOA.

The situation is probably no different in many Irish firms: the union plays a reactive not proactive role.[14] Individual unions and employers should recognise the validity and usefulness of a consensual approach to issues like sexual harassment. That consen-

---

[13] The ICTU recommend in a passage worth quoting in full: "As sexual harassment is often linked to the woman's status in the employment hierarchy, policies to deal with sexual harassment are more effective when they are included in an overall policy to promote equal opportunities and to improve the position of women. Also, a procedure to deal with complaints of sexual harassment should be regarded as only one component of a strategy to deal with the problem. The prime objective should be to change behaviour and attitudes to prevent sexual harassment". *Working Women and Europe: Recommendations and Code of Practice on Sexual Harassment* (Dublin: ICTU, undated), leaflet 3. A similar opinion is advanced in the Irish *Code of Practice* as follows: "In order to deal with the problem of sexual harassment in employment, employers should develop strategies aimed at prevention and accessible complaints procedures. Experience has shown that such measures are most effective when integrated into broader equal opportunities policies", *Code of Practice, op. cit.*, page 11.

[14] Mandate and the ICTU's Construction Industry Committee, for example, have concluded agreements on policies with Superquinn and the Construction Industry Federation, respectively.

sus should stem from a recognition that the employer and trade union have a common interest in limiting incidences of sexual harassment in the workplace, as well as from an acknowledgement of the positive contribution that unions can make. The latter can stem from using the trade union as an invaluable source of advice.

The ICTU has published a wealth of information on sexual harassment and will assist member unions in drawing up policies. Further, employees are more likely to accept and abide by policies to which their unions have contributed. All of this information can be presented to a reluctant employer, though it may take some hard negotiating by the union for an employer to acknowledge the need for union involvement.

THE ROLE OF THE SHOP STEWARD

Thus far, we have dealt with the responsibility of the union as an organisation with respect to sexual harassment and employment equality, first within their own organisations, and then in dealing with employers. In this section, the role of the shop steward is examined (see Figure 6.1 at the end of the chapter).

At a minimum, a shop steward should be versed in all aspects of the law and organisational/union policy on sexual harassment. In addition to circulating union policy, shop stewards can ensure that memos are sent to all members explaining and reiterating the union's concern with the issue. Meetings provide another opportunity to communicate the union's policy on sexual harassment and are often better than the cold-hearted, and often ignored, circular. By whatever means, the shop steward has to make sure that all members understand what sexual harassment is and what it is not. Members have to know that it is wrong (and why it is wrong) and what to do if they wish to make a complaint. Communication is thus important, not least for providing basic information on sexual harassment, but also to raise awareness about the issue, particularly in environments which have traditionally had largely male workforces.

Communication is also a two-way process: shop stewards have to listen to members. As Noirín Greene, Equality Officer with

SIPTU, writing on behalf of SIPTU's National Women's Committee, warns:

> The absence of reported complaints about sexual harassment in the workplace does not mean that it does not exist. The very nature of sexual harassment means that employees will often be reluctant to complain.[15]

Shop stewards therefore have to be attentive to members' needs, and be aware of the complexity and subtlety of the issues surrounding sexual harassment.

Dealing with a Complaint of Sexual Harassment

If a member claims she is being sexual harassed, a shop steward should not ignore the problem or trivialise it with statements like "it's only the lads having a bit of fun", or "don't worry about it, it will go away". Instead, he or she should be understanding of, and comforting to, the individual. The individual should be informed that she was right to raise the matter, and that the union will support her. If the allegation warrants further action, the shop steward should help the person put the allegation in writing and to substantiate the claim. The shop steward can also, if deemed necessary, talk to other workers. Indeed, SIPTU advises shop stewards to talk discreetly to other members to see if they have experienced similar problems.[16] If the shop steward is unsure as to what to do, he or she should consult the full-time union official.

SIPTU advises further that the claimant should be asked as to what she wants done. For example, the individual may prefer to keep the issue private. Alternatively, she may wish for the shop steward to take action by either talking to the alleged harasser or management or both.

If the allegation of harassment is serious, a shop steward should be wary of trying to resolve the problem by talking to the accused, regardless of whether he is a union member or not. A shop steward has to be aware that his role is of representation, not management. Therefore, he should inform management and

---

[15] SIPTU, "Sexual Harassment is no Joke", *op. cit.*, page 4.

[16] *Ibid.*, page 8 .

request that they take action. What that action is will depend much on the policies of the organisation and the nature of the allegation. If the shop steward, or indeed the complainant, is not satisfied as to the way the complaint is dealt with by management, he may, in consultation with the full-time branch official, raise the issue with management in further negotiations, or alternatively, as the final course of action, pursue a claim externally.

Until the allegation is proved correct, a shop steward has to treat it as just that, an allegation not proof. Regardless of his personal feelings and knowledge of the situation, the steward has to act professionally and fairly. He has to ensure that the complaint is properly handled, and, if justified, that something be done about the harassment.

Not all complaints are made first to the shop steward. In many cases, a woman makes an allegation of sexual harassment to a manager, and an investigation, however informal, is begun. The union is then informed of that investigation. A shop steward should not criticise the individual for going directly to management, and thus avoiding the union in making a grievance. Instead, he should offer her advice and support and reserve judgement until the facts of the case are known. As SIPTU advises, the shop steward should do his best to limit any further stress to, and certainly victimisation of, the complainant. He may also impress upon management the need for a prompt, but thorough, investigation.

It is not uncommon to find cases where both the victim and the harasser are union members. Whether they are members of the same union, or of different unions matters little, just that they are both entitled to representation if they request it. The practise in such cases is to inform both the harasser and the victim that they are entitled to union representation. The AFL-CIO in America caution unions about over-reacting:

> The union has the duty to represent all its members. When a member accuses another member of harassment, some unions assign different representatives for each member. The union has

the right to say there is no merit and to decline to pursue a case of either side. [17]

On the other hand, Rubenstein reports on the practice of certain unions in Britain, notably the ATGWU (Amalgamated Transport and General Workers Union), to refuse representation to alleged harassers. He states:

> There is a growing view that sexual harassment of one member by another involves a breach of the perpetrator's terms of membership and provides grounds for the union to refuse to act on his behalf.[18]

Therefore, a union representative may have to make the decision to represent or not represent the alleged harasser as well as the complainant. The practice tends to be to provide equal representation.

SUMMARY

Despite what some may think, there is much a union can do to limit sexual harassment in the workplace. To be more specific, a trade union should encourage employers to adopt policies on sexual harassment, they should work in conjunction with employers in developing such policies, they should be involved in communicating that policy and they should, finally, encourage workers both to use and to abide by that policy. Unions officials have to receive proper training and be encouraged to talk to members. In talking with members, officials have to get across the view that sexual harassment is wrong and won't be tolerated, and that union members who continue to harass women will be penalised.

Sexual harassment can provide many problems for unions. In unions where the bulk of the membership is male, and where tradition is entrenched, there may not be a great awareness of the need to do something about sexual harassment. Further, problems for unions can be compounded many times over when an accusation is made by one union member against another. These

---

[17] AFL-CIO, *op cit.*, page 6.

[18] Michael Rubenstein, "Preventing and Remedying Sexual Harassment at Work, A Resource Manual", 1989, Industrial Relations Service, page 25.

reasons — apathy or ignorance on the part of membership, coupled with the likelihood of representing a harasser — should not deter a union from action. Indeed, the norm in recent years seem very much to come down on the side of trade unions. Led by the ICTU, many trade unions, and especially those with large female membership, have taken strong stands against sexual harassment. They have encouraged employers to adopt policies, and for members to respect that policy. They have educated workers, members and non-members alike, about sexual harassment and in so doing raised awareness about the issue. Their record finally in representing workers is very good. The fact that most cases that go to the Labour Court involve non-union companies is testimony in no small part to the role that unions play in voicing workers' opinions at the workplace. Regardless of whether a law is passed in the coming year on sexual harassment, trade unions are likely to continue this important duty.

Figure 6.1: What Should A Shop Steward Do

1. Know the law, as well as company and union policy on sexual harassment. Inform all workers about it.

2. Make all your members aware of their rights, particularly the right to an environment free of harassment. Inform members of the procedures to follow in making a complaint.

3. When a member comes to you with a complaint, do not ignore or trivialise the issue. Instead, take time to listen to what the person is saying. Be empathic, sympathetic and helpful. Advise the individual of her rights.

4. Have the complaint recorded in writing, and present it to management. Insist if necessary on anonymity and confidentiality and that management take all the necessary steps to investigate the complaint. Make sure that the complainant is not victimised.

5. Finally, follow up. Make sure the outcome is positive.

CHAPTER SEVEN

HOW TO BRING A SEXUAL HARASSMENT CLAIM

If you find yourself being sexually harassed I would advise you to summon up the courage to tell your union representative, senior management, members of your family, the EEA, etc., what the problem is and, if all else fails, report it to the police.[1]

INTRODUCTION

Given the serious negative impact which sexual harassment can have on both the victim and the employer,[2] incidents of sexual harassment cannot be ignored by either party. Rather, they must be dealt with as quickly and efficiently as possible. In that context, then, this chapter explains how a victim of sexual harassment should set about tackling the problem, from the initial stages of documenting incidents of sexual harassment and complaining to management, right through to bringing a case before an Equality Officer, the Labour Court or a court of law. Given the modern trend in other jurisdictions of referring sexual harassment cases to alternative dispute resolution processes, concepts such as arbitration and mediation are also discussed.

RECOGNISING AND DOCUMENTING HARASSMENT

The first, and sometimes most difficult, step for any victim of sexual harassment on the road to bringing a claim against her employer is for her to recognise that she is actually being harassed.

---

[1] Siobhán Butler, "The Silent Witness", *Evening Press*, 12 April 1995. Ms Butler was a victim of sexual harassment.

[2] *Cf.* Chapter 1.

Many victims simply attempt to ignore the problem by convincing themselves that they are over-reacting to harmless jokes or pranks. Ideally, a victim should:

- Remind herself that anybody can be sexually harassed, and that she is not in any way responsible for her harasser's conduct.[3]

- Remember that the Department of Equality and Law Reform's *Code of Practice* provides that it is the reaction of the victim rather than the intention of the harasser which determines whether or not an action or actions constitute sexual harassment.[4]

- Telephone the Employment Equality Agency for an informal conversation. The Agency should be able to clarify whether or not the conduct in question constitutes sexual harassment.[5]

- Inform her family, friends and colleagues, where possible.

- Keep a written record of each incident, detailing when and where it took place, what was said or done and who was present.

In addition, the victim should point out to the harasser that his words or conduct are not appreciated. Ideally, he should be told in simple but firm terms that his comments or actions are both unwelcome and inappropriate. Sometimes it may be easier to repel an unwanted advance with a jocose rebuff, but if the harasser either fails, or refuses, to get the message, he should be clearly warned off. In most cases, the harassment will stop at that point. Unfortunately, however, it may go further. If the harasser does continue to make unwelcome comments, the victim should make a formal complaint to management.

---

[3] *Ibid.*

[4] Department of Equality and Law Reform, *Code of Practice: Measures to Protect the Dignity of Women and Men at Work* (Dublin, 1994), 10. See also Chapter Two.

[5] The victim need not disclose her name, although it may later be of benefit if she asks the Agency to note her name and the nature of the query.

MAKING A COMPLAINT

If a victim of sexual harassment decides to make a formal complaint about her harasser's conduct, it should be made to somebody who has responsibility for, or control over, him. In larger companies the victim may choose to approach the equal opportunities officer, personnel officer or employee assistance officer. In other cases it may be more appropriate to approach the harasser's supervisor, the floor manager or the office manager. If the victim is uncertain or worried about approaching the individual to whom she should complain, it may be of assistance to contact her trade union representative or to bring a female colleague with her when she is registering her complaint. Regardless of the approach the victim decides to take, her complaint should be taken seriously and handled in a confidential manner. If the employer, manager or supervisor to whom the complaint is made fails to deal with the matter in such a manner, the victim should immediately look for assistance from outside the company by approaching either the Employment Equality Agency or her union representative.

To their credit, a growing number of companies have put formal sexual harassment complaints procedures in place over the last ten years. Many of them have either appointed equal opportunities officers or made specific employees responsible for dealing with complaints.[6] Unfortunately, such model organisations remain in the minority. Most companies, particularly very small firms, have not implemented sexual harassment policies. For that reason, supervisors and mangers have neither the training nor the experience necessary to deal with complaints. Similarly, they have no guidelines to follow and are in a far from ideal position to deal with the problem. In such situations, complaints should be made at the highest possible level of the firm. Alternatively, the complaint may have to be made outside the firm.

It can be particularly difficult to complain where one is employed in a small firm or by a sole trader and the harasser is one's employer. While improper comments or sexual advances must still be immediately rebuffed, if at all possible, the victim should

---

[6] Cf. Chapter Four.

bring a friend or a trade union official with her when she goes to make an official complaint.

Regardless of the circumstances, the victim should, once again, keep a written record of what was said by both parties when the formal complaint was made. If possible, she should get somebody who was present at the time to verify her account of the meeting, even going so far as to get that witness to sign her summary.

The complainant's first option, however, in so far as is possible, must be to use any internal complaints procedure provided by the company. In so doing the complainant not only allows the company an opportunity to resolve the matter quickly and satisfactorily, but also ensures that the Labour Court will not find in favour of the employer at any subsequent hearing because of her failure to try to resolve the dispute in such a manner.

The fact that a company does not have a policy on sexual harassment does not preclude an individual from making a complaint. In such instances, victims of harassment should use the company's standard internal grievance procedure or, in the absence of such a procedure, complain to an appropriate superior officer. If the initial complaint does not lead to a satisfactory outcome then, and only then, should a complaint be registered with the Labour Court.

SOURCES OF HELP

Making a formal complaint can be a nerve-wracking experience for even the most confident and out-going of complainants. Given that such is the case, the complainant should consider asking her trade union representative, or her union's equality officer, to accompany her when she goes to register her complaint. Not only will the union representative provide moral support, but he or she will usually be of considerable assistance in guiding the complainant through the entire process as well as explaining what needs to be done and why. The final advantage for the complainant of involving her union representative at such an early stage is that the official will be familiar with the details of the case should they subsequently need to represent the victim before an Equality Officer or the Labour Court.

There are two other options for victims of sexual harassment. The first is to seek assistance from the Employment Equality Agency. The Agency has been at the forefront of the drive towards eliminating workplace sexual harassment in this jurisdiction and has built up a wealth of experience and expertise in the area over the last ten years. Its services are provided free of charge and on a confidential basis. While the Agency is unlikely to be able to provide the same individual assistance and attention as may be available from the complainant's trade union, it is always advisable to discuss the matter with them before pursuing a case before the Labour Court.

The second alternative to approaching one's trade union is to go to a solicitor for professional legal advice and, if necessary, representation. There are three main advantages inherent in obtaining the services of a solicitor. The first is that a solicitor who is well versed in labour law will be able to clearly explain the legal ramifications of what has happened, as well as the options which are open to a victim of sexual harassment who is seeking legal redress against her employer. The second is that the involvement of a solicitor in the case may encourage the complainant's employer to resolve the matter at an early stage or to offer a greater sum by way of compensation. The third advantage is that one can be certain that a solicitor, unlike one's union, has no conflict of interests. Rather, his or her only objective should be to resolve the matter in the best interests of the victim.

A number of other factors should, however, be borne in mind by any victim of sexual harassment who is considering approaching a solicitor. The first is that very few solicitors have an in-depth knowledge of sexual harassment law. Generally speaking, both full-time trade union officials and the staff of the Employment Equality Agency will have more relevant expertise. For that reason, any complainant who intends to obtain the services of a solicitor should ensure that the solicitor in question practices labour law. One's trade union official should be able to suggest an appropriate solicitor who has established a good reputation and can offer a sympathetic ear, moral support and sound advice. The second problem is that most solicitors will charge quite substantial fees, whereas both the complainant's trade union and the

Employment Equality Agency provide their services free of charge. The best course of action is to shop around for the solicitor who will provide the necessary services for the lowest fee. The complainant should also check whether or not her union membership entitles her to free legal services from a solicitor affiliated to the union.

EQUALITY OFFICERS

If a dispute relating to an incident or incidents of sexual harassment is not resolved to the satisfaction of the complainant at company level by way of a formal investigation or otherwise, the main option available to that complainant is to bring a case before a Labour Relations Commission Equality Officer or the Labour Court under the Employment Equality Act, 1977.[7]

The Labour Relations Commission was established in January, 1991 under section 24 of the Industrial Relations Act, 1990. The Commission has general responsibility for the promotion of good industrial relations through the provision of a comprehensive range of industrial relations services.[8] One of those services is the Commission's Equality Service which had previously operated under the auspices of the Labour Court. Equality Officers, who are permanent, full-time, civil servants seconded to the Commission, investigate disputes under the Anti-Discrimination (Pay) Act, 1974, and the Employment Equality Act, 1977, and issue recommendations on those disputes.[9] Despite their civil service status, equality officers are independent in respect of the exercise of their functions and are free to determine their own procedures.

Approaching the Equality Service is a particularly attractive option for both complainants and employers for three main reasons. The first is that Equality Officers conduct their investigations in private and, for that reason, cases with which they deal tend to attract little publicity. The second attraction of the service is that Equality Officers conduct their investigations in an infor-

---

[7] See sections 19, *et seq*.

[8] Labour Relations Commission, The Labour Relations Commission, (Dublin, 1992), 2.

[9] Labour Relations Commission, *op. cit.*, 9.

mal manner which is unlikely to be as intimidating as either a full hearing of the Labour Court or litigation in a court of law. The third and final benefit is that Equality Officers have a long track record of producing sound, erudite recommendations which show a better understanding of the legal principles involved in sexual harassment cases than has been displayed by the Labour Court.

An individual who is considering approaching the Equality Service should, however, bear two further factors in mind. First, an Equality Officer's recommendation is not, in and of itself, legally binding on the parties,[10] while the second is that a party who is dissatisfied with the recommendation may appeal it to the Labour Court.[11] For those reasons many complainants find it easier to steer away from the Equality Service and initiate their cases in the Labour Court.

THE LABOUR COURT

The Labour Court is an independent tri-partite body which was established under the Industrial Relations Act, 1946, as a court of last resort in the process of industrial relations dispute resolution. The Court's functions have, however, since been redefined by the Industrial Relations Acts, 1969, 1976 and 1990. The Court has also been allocated further responsibilities under the Anti-Discrimination (Pay) Act, 1974, and the Employment Equality Act, 1977.

At present, the Court consists of a Chairman, three Deputy Chairmen and eight ordinary members, all of whom are appointed by the Minister for Enterprise and Employment. The eight ordinary members are, however, appointed on the basis of nominations made by organisations representing trade unions and employers' organisations.

When considering a case, the Court may consist of the Chairman and all the ordinary members, or a Chairman (who may be

---

[10] Although the party seeking to enforce the recommendation may appeal to the Labour Court for "a determination that the recommendation has not been implemented." See section 21(1) of the 1977 Act.

[11] See section 21 of the 1977 Act.

one of the Deputy Chairmen) and two ordinary members (one trade union representative and one employers' representative). Only the members of the Court constituted to hear a case have the right to vote on that case. Where the members of the Court are unable to agree on how the matter before them should be determined, section 20 of the 1946 Act provides that the matter should be determined in accordance with the wishes of the majority of ordinary members or, in default of such an agreement, in accordance with the wishes of all the members. On the rare occasions on which there is no such majority, the matter is determined in accordance with the opinion of the Chairman. The decision of the Court is pronounced by the Chairman and no indication is given of the existence of any other opinion, whether assenting or dissenting.

Proceedings brought before the Labour Court are unlike those before a court of law in that they are informal in nature. The Court may, however, summon witnesses before it, examine those witnesses on oath and require them to produce for its inspection any documentation in their possession or control. Despite the fact that the Court has such powers, it is extremely unusual for parties appearing before it to be represented by solicitors or barristers. Complainants in sexual harassment cases who intend to pursue their cases before the Labour Court are best advised to have their trade union representative act for them as the official in question will, almost certainly, have more experience in dealing with the Court than most lawyers. Similarly, employers who are members of IBEC should consider asking that organisation to represent them before the Court.

Unlike an Equality Officer's recommendation, a determination of the Labour Court is binding on the parties to a sexual harassment case. It may, however, be appealed to the High Court on a point of law within forty-two days of the date on which it was issued.[12]

Victims of sexual harassment should note that Section 19(5) of the 1977 Act provides that:

---

[12] See section 21(2)(d) of the 1977 Act.

Save only where reasonable cause can be shown, a reference [to the Labour Court] shall be lodged not later than six months from the date of the first occurrence of the act alleged to constitute the discrimination.

A victim should therefore avoid any undue delay in initiating her claim and ensure that any party or parties acting on her behalf take all the necessary steps within the limitation period prescribed in the legislation.

PROVING A CASE

The greatest single problem encountered by a complainant is proving her case. Allegations of sexual harassment have a tendency to be difficult to prove, in that incidents of harassment most often occur when there are no third parties or potential witnesses around.[13] Even where third parties do witness the conduct about which the victim is complaining, it can be difficult to persuade them to testify against their employers. Proving that an incident of sexual harassment actually occurred is made even more difficult by the fact that sexual harassment allegations are usually made some time after the harassment began. In such cases, the victim may have mislaid any documentary evidence,[14] witnesses may have died, left the company and become untraceable or simply forgotten important details. As Flynn explains:

---

[13] According to IBEC, the Labour Court will take into account the creditability of each party where there is a lack of collaborative evidence. The Court's conclusions will be "influenced by the detail and consistency of the evidence presented by both sides. If the claimant's evidence is consistent and detailed and the respondent's evidence is vague about matters which he or she should have been expected to recall then their testimony is less compelling. The Equality Officer and Labour Court will also [check whether or not] the claimant mentioned the alleged harassment to work colleagues." IBEC, *Guidelines on Sexual Harassment*, (Dublin).

[14] Employers may find it easier to bring incontrovertible documentary evidence before the Court. Such evidence should include copies of any policy on sexual harassment implemented by the employer, records relating to any internal investigation into the complainant's allegations, circulars or memoranda on sexual harassment which were issued to employees and, if appropriate, relevant personnel records.

There are recurring difficulties for complainants in sexual harassment cases, chief of which is the difficulty of proving that the
incidents which are alleged to have taken place did in fact occur.
As the Labour Court itself noted regarding the evidence produced in *A Company v A Worker*, "[a]s is common in cases of alleged sexual harassment there is no direct corroborative evidence that many of the incidents complained of actually took
place". It then went on to note another, and possibly more trou-
bling, feature of such cases, namely the difficulty in establishing
what was the significance of the events which are agreed, or
have been proved, to have occurred. It said that "[i]n relation to
those [incidents] acknowledged by the company, there is conflicting evidence as to their context, and as to whether the worker
clearly indicated that she regarded them as offensive." This
problem, the production of meaning of agreed events, is in some
ways central to the legal treatment of sexual harassment.[15]

For these reasons it is extremely important that complainants
keep the kind of written records which have already been referred
to earlier in this chapter.

DEFENDING A CASE[16]

In defending sexual harassment cases before Equality Officers or
the Labour Court, employers will usually adopt one or more of the
three basic defences to such claims. The first, and most obvious, of
those defence strategies is to deny that the incident or incidents
alleged by the complainant ever happened. Alternatively, the
employer may acknowledge that the incident or incidents did in
fact occur, but only in the context of a consensual relationship between the employees involved. These approaches ensure that the
complainant has to formally prove that the alleged conduct actually occurred — an onus which, as has already been pointed
out, is not easily discharged. It is not, however, in the best interests of an employer to adopt such an approach to a case if it is

---

[15] Leo Flynn, "Privileged Perceptions in Sexual Harassment Law", (1994) 12
Irish Law Times (n.s.) 14.

[16] *Cf.* Chapter 3.

quite obvious that the complainant was harassed. Rather, the employer should move on to adopt an alternative defence.

The second of the three primary defences available to a company is to argue that even if the complainant was sexually harassed, it is not vicariously liable because the harasser was acting outside the "scope of his employment."[17] While the Labour Court would not seem to be overly receptive to such arguments, the defence in question has been recognised by the High Court[18] and should be accepted by the Labour Court in appropriate circumstances if it is to comply with its obligation to abide by and apply principles mapped out by courts of law.

The third defence available to employers is to argue that they took all reasonable steps to prevent their employees from being sexually harassed and that they acted quickly to put an end to the harassment in question once they became aware that it had been occurring. This defence should be available to any company which has taken a responsible approach to the issue of sexual harassment as it will have agreed and implemented a sexual harassment policy, advertised it in the workplace, provided appropriate training to supervisors and managers and investigated any complaint in an appropriate manner.[19] In such circumstances it is extremely unlikely that the Labour Court would find any employer vicariously liable.

ALTERNATIVE APPROACHES

As was explained in Chapter Two, the application of Catherine MacKinnon's sex discrimination thesis in Irish law necessarily involves a somewhat strained approach to interpreting the Employment Equality Act, 1977, in the same way as English and American courts are required to adopt expansive, and occasionally inexplicable, interpretations of the legislation applicable in those jurisdictions. Quite predictably, these strained interpreta-

---

[17] Cf. Chapter 3.

[18] See the discussion of the decision of Mr. Justice Costello in *The Health Board v. B.C. and the Labour Court*, unreported, High Court, 19 January 1994, in Chapter 3.

[19] Cf. Chapters 4 and 5.

tions of sex discrimination legislation cannot cover certain types of cases. For that reason, some victims of sexual harassment and their lawyers have attempted to tackle the problem in forums other than the Labour Court.

The Employment Appeals Tribunal

The main alternative to going to the Labour Court is to bring an unfair dismissals action against one's employer in the Employment Appeals Tribunal under the Unfair Dismissals Acts, 1977-1993.[20] Such an approach is suitable both where the victim has been dismissed because she would not comply with her employer's sexual demands and where she resigned on the basis that his conduct left her with no other choice. Any such resignation is likely to be deemed to constitute a "constructive dismissal" and comes within the ambit of the Unfair Dismissals Acts. The Acts in question, however, preclude a significant number of categories of employees from claiming to have been unfairly dismissed. The main categories of employees excluded by the Acts are:

- Those who have less than one year's continuous service with the employer who dismissed them;[21]

- Those who have reached the normal retiring age for employees of the same employer in similar employment;

- Civil servants;

- Officers of Health Boards and VECs;

- Persons employed by close relatives, who are members of their employer's household and are employed at a private dwellinghouse or a farm in or on which both the employee and the employer reside;

---

[20] See, generally, Adrian F. Twomey, "Work and the Law", in Noel Harvey, *Effective Supervisory Management in Ireland*, (Dublin: NCIR Press, 1994), 243, at 258-262.

[21] Except where the employee concerned was dismissed because of her involvement in trade union activities, pregnancy or matters related thereto. In addition, s.3(b) of the 1993 Act prevents employers from seeking to avoid the application of the Acts by employing workers under a succession of short, fixed-term contracts.

- Members of the Gardaí and Permanent Defence Forces;

- FÁS trainees.

Somewhat unusually, however, the 1993 Act provides that an employee may bring an unfair dismissals action against her employer even if her contract of service is in breach of the tax or social welfare codes.[22]

If an employer is to avoid liability under the Unfair Dismissals Acts he or she must be able to prove to the Tribunal that the dismissal resulted "wholly or mainly" from reasons relating to the employees capability, qualifications, competence, conduct, redundancy, or other substantial grounds. Similarly, a dismissal is not considered to have been unfair if the continuance of the employee in the job would have resulted in the breach of a provision in a statute or statutory instrument. For that reason, a complainant in a sexual harassment case will win that case before the Tribunal if she can prove that she was dismissed and her employer is unable to prove that the dismissal was for one of the reasons mentioned above.

The most common ground which employers seek to rely on when attempting to justify a dismissal is that of misconduct. The nature of the misconduct must be such that it undermines the relationship of trust, which the law regards as being necessary between an employer and his or her employee. Even minor acts of misconduct may suffice if they breach that relationship. In grounding his or her defence upon conduct grounds, however, an employer will usually seek to pin the dismissal on a single act of gross misconduct or a series of less significant acts followed by a series of warnings.

A complainant has six months from the date of the dismissal within which to initiate her claim and may choose to have her case heard either by a Rights Commissioner or the Employment

---

[22] Such contracts are usually regarded as being unenforceable on public policy grounds.

Appeals Tribunal.[23] The Commissioner or Tribunal, if satisfied that the claimant has been unfairly dismissed, can opt to award her one of three specific remedies. The first is reinstatement, in which case the victim is legally deemed never to have been dismissed. She simply goes back into her job and is entitled to receive back pay. The second remedy is re-engagement, which involves her returning to the same or a similar position. Unlike reinstatement, however, re-engagement involves the employee losing her seniority and accumulated rights. The third, and most commonly awarded, remedy is financial compensation. Such compensation is limited to a maximum of 104 weeks remuneration, although the maximum sum is rarely awarded.

The Civil Courts

The overwhelming majority of complainants in cases involving sexual harassment will, if they choose to pursue the matter, initiate cases in either the Labour Court or the Employment Appeals Tribunal rather than opting to sue their employers in courts of law. It is, however, worth noting that complainants have the option of taking that route in an attempt to secure more substantial compensation than has traditionally been awarded by the Labour Court.

In *Butler v. Four Star Pizza (Ireland) Ltd.,*[24] for example, the plaintiff had been both physically and verbally sexually harassed by a pizza delivery man in the employment of the company. When she complained to the manager he "just laughed."[25] Despite repeated complaints the delivery man's conduct continued unabated. Ms. Butler eventually left the company and reported the matter to the Employment Equality Agency who did not pursue it as far as the Labour Court. She then approached a solicitor who advised her to take the unusual step of suing the defendant com-

---

[23] If, however, the employer objects to the case being heard by a Rights Commissioner it must go to the Employment Appeals Tribunal instead. See Section 8(3), Unfair Dismissals Act, 1977.

[24] Unreported, Mr. Justice Spain, Circuit Court, 2 March, 1995.

[25] "Alleged sexual harassment victim threatened 'to use a knife'", *The Irish Times,* 9 February 1995.

pany in the Circuit Court for breach of contract or wrongful repudiation of her contract.

The result was, in an Irish context, spectacularly successful, with the President of the Circuit Court awarding the plaintiff £10,000 — a sum far in excess of what Ms. Butler might have expected to have been awarded had her case been heard by the Labour Court under the Employment Equality Act, 1977. Observing that no action had been taken by management in respect of the harassment, Mr. Justice Spain held that the plaintiff "was justified in leaving her employment where a situation had arisen which she could not reasonably be expected to tolerate."[26]

Despite Ms. Butler's success in the Circuit Court, victims of sexual harassment may not be overly anxious to follow her approach as breach of contract actions can be complicated, time-consuming and costly. They do, however, provide an alternative to the traditional route to obtaining compensation and are certainly worth considering in circumstances similar to those surrounding Ms. Butler's case.[27] Similarly, victims of physical harassment may wish to consider the option of suing their assailants for the tort of battery or their employers on the basis that they may be vicariously liable for such battery.

Arbitration

While they would not appear to have gained any significant foothold in Ireland in the context of sexual harassment disputes, there are a number of dispute resolution processes other than litigation which have been successfully used by victims of harassment in other countries. Perhaps the best known of those alternative methods of dispute resolution is arbitration, which is defined by Brown and Marriott as being:

> a private mechanism for the resolution of disputes which takes place in private pursuant to an agreement between two or more parties, under which the parties agree to be bound by the deci-

---

[26] "Girl sexually pawed at work gets £10,000", *The Irish Independent,* 3 March 1995.

[27] See Figure 7.1.

sion to be given by the arbitrator according to law after a fair hearing, such decision being enforceable by law.[28]

Any dispute or claim concerning legal rights which can be the subject of an enforceable award is capable of being settled by arbitration[29] and, significantly, the awards of arbitrators are, if properly made, enforceable in the courts under section 41 of the Arbitration Act, 1954.[30]

Arbitration can be an attractive option for employers in that it is invariably faster and cheaper than litigation, while it also ensures that the details of a claim do not become public knowledge or the focus of media attention. For that reason, employers may, on occasion, find it worthwhile to include a clause in the contracts of new employees which requires the parties to resolve any future disputes relating to sexual harassment by means of arbitration.

Parties who are interested in going to arbitration may appoint any mutually acceptable individual as arbitrator, although it is often advisable initially to approach the Chartered Institute of Arbitrators who will recommend appropriate, professionally qualified arbitrators.

Mediation

The preferred option for both complainants and management in many sexual harassment cases in the United States is no longer that of litigation, or processes which are largely similar to litigation such as arbitration. Rather, the parties seek to resolve their disputes through mediation. In the words of Brown and Marriott:

> [m]ediation is a facilitative process in which disputing parties engage the assistance of a neutral third party who acts as a me-

---

[28] Henry, J. Brown and Arthur L. Marriott, *ADR Principles and Practice*, (London: Sweet and Maxwell, 1993), 56.

[29] Sir Michael J. Mustill and Stewart C. Boyd, *The Law and Practice of Commercial Arbitration in England, 2nd ed.,* (London: Butterworths, 1989), 149.

[30] Section 41 provides that "[a]n award on an arbitration agreement may, by leave of the Court, be enforced in the same manner as a judgement or order to the same effect and, where leave is so given, judgement may be entered in terms of the award." See also the judgement of Mr. Justice McCarthy of the Supreme Court in *Keenan v. Shield Insurance Co. Ltd.,* (1989) I.R. 89, at 96.

diator in their dispute. The neutral has no authority to make any decisions which are binding on them, but uses certain procedures, techniques and skills to help them to negotiate a resolution of their dispute by agreement without adjudication. . . . Mediation differs from arbitration in that the role of the neutral third party in arbitration is to consider the issues and then to make a decision which determines the issues and is binding on the parties. The neutral third party in mediation does not have any authority to make any decision for the parties, nor is that the mediator's role or function.[31]

Mediation has been described as the "sleeping giant" of Alternative Dispute Resolution (ADR)[32] and is certainly an option which is worth considering because of its numerous advantages. As MacMahon points out:

> Mediation allows the parties themselves to retain control of, and participate more actively in, the outcome/settlement. The mediation process restores communication and builds trust. It breaks impasses by dispelling unverified assumptions and unrealistic expectations. The mediator who is a facilitator, not a decision maker, helps to eliminate problems of ego and personality. Mediated solutions tend to be "win-win" and not "win-lose". Mediation is private, quick, cost effective, flexible and informal. It helps to preserve the relationship between the parties, where relevant. Most importantly, mediation works. National statistics of United States Arbitration and Mediation Inc. indicate a settlement rate of 80 per cent to 85 per cent of cases using mediation.[33]

In sexual harassment cases mediation has the particular advantage of helping to ensure that complainants can have their cases resolved without having to resort to an adversarial method of dispute resolution. Such methods usually damage the relationships between employers and employees to such an extent that they

---

[31] Brown and Marriott, *op. cit.*, 108.

[32] J.F. Henry and J.K. Lieberman, *The Manager's Guide to Resolving Legal Disputes: Better Results without Litigation*, (New York: Harper and Row, 1985).

[33] Brian MacMahon, "Mediation — Could it make your practice more profitable?" (1994) *Incorporated Law Society Gazette* 379.

almost inevitably come to an end. Because mediation is concilia-
tory in nature and attempts to avoid confrontation, the process
stands a particularly good chance of both resolving the dispute
and enabling the complainant to return to the workplace without
having severely damaged her relationship with her employer. As
American mediation guru John Haynes explains:

> The outcome of a successful mediation is an agreement that is
> satisfactory to all the disputants. The agreement addresses the
> problem with a mutually acceptable solution and is structured in
> a way that helps to maintain the relationships of all the people
> involved.[34]

While one does not need to be legally represented at a mediation
hearing, complainants should bear in mind the fact that the employer is likely to be represented by a management team as well
as by legal or IBEC representatives. For that reason, the complainant should attempt to ensure that she is at least accompanied by her trade union representative. The trend in the United
States is towards having full legal teams at mediation sessions.
The problem with doing so, however, is that such an approach to
the mediation process tends not only to obviate the primary advantage of mediation, but also decreases the likelihood of reaching a mutually acceptable settlement.

Should one ultimately decide to go to mediation, the Mediators'
Institute of Ireland should be able to recommend an appropriate
mediator.

Pressing Criminal Charges

It is worth remembering that some acts of sexual harassment are
not only unlawful but are also criminal offences. For that reason,
victims of particularly serious forms of sexual harassment may, in
addition to pursuing a private suit against their employers, also
seek to have their harassers charged with the commission of
criminal charges, such as rape, statutory rape or aggravated sexual assault. In such cases, the victim should contact the Gardaí

---

[34] John M. Haynes, Thelma Fisher and Richard Greenslade, *Alternative Dispute Resolution: Fundamentals of Family Mediation*, (Horsmonden, Kent:
Old Bailey Press, 1993), 1.

Síochána who will pursue the matter if they are of the opinion that an offence has been committed.

Figure 7.1: Case-study — Siobhán Butler[35]

In her recent letter to Postbag, Kathleen Connolly of the Employment Equality Agency (EEA) made the point that most complaints of sexual harassment brought to their attention are resolved to the satisfaction of all concerned without formal use of legal proceedings, etc.

She probably meant that the problem is resolved to the satisfaction of management and victim insofar that agreement is reached that the circumstances which gave rise to the sexual harassment in the first place should not arise again in that workplace. If management do not co-operate with the EEA, then the problem of sexual harassment cannot be resolved at the EEA level.

In the absence of an independent witness willing to give evidence in a court of law, a victim of sexual harassment is at a severe disadvantage in attempting to prove her case there.

Even if the act is seen by a number of independent witnesses, experience has shown that there is great difficulty in getting them to give evidence in open court because of the attendant wide publicity such cases receive from the media. That same publicity also causes much distress to the families of both victim and abuser. For that reason court proceedings should only be taken as a last resort by the victim.

In such cases there are essentially three parties involved — the victim, the abuser, and the management who failed to take steps to stop the abuse. The media focus their attention on the interaction between the victim and the abuser and give little publicity to the failures of the management which allow such situations to continue.

In her letter to Postbag Kathleen Connolly made reference to a woman who left her job because of sexual harassment and was awarded £10,000 by the Circuit Court. I am that woman and I can

---

[35] Siobhán Butler, *op. cit.* Siobhán Butler was the plaintiff in *Butler v. Four Star Pizza Ltd.*, *op. cit.*

assure you that being awarded £10,000 and actually getting the awarded sum of money are two very distinct things.

The inference in Kathleen Connolly's letter was that sexual harassment cases such as mine could be dealt with in a satisfactory manner by the EEA. If that had been the case there would have been no need for me to have my case heard in the Circuit Court.

Ms. Connolly was not aware when she prepared her letter that I had first pursued my case via the EEA, which took the case in hand in October, 1991. After a period of months had elapsed the EEA then found that it no longer had the power to deal with the case.

The explanation I was given at the time was that the EEA was statute-barred after a period of six months from pursuing the case if the parties concerned — management and the victim — did not allow the EEA to hear the case within that period of time. This is still one of the restraints within which the EEA has to operate.

In my case the response from my former employers was received by the EEA on April 2, 1992 — this was approximately three weeks outside the six month limit within which the EEA operates. At this stage I think that it would be fair to observe that I do not know who dragged their heels in getting my problem resolved at that stage — the EEA or my former employers.

Many people who are initially prepared to complain of their problem of sexual harassment get discouraged by the bureaucracy, the delays, and the nasty innuendoes the receive from people in sheltered environments, and give up the fight. At this stage I can understand their position only too well and have the greatest sympathy for their predicament.

Following my frustrating experience with the EEA and my former employer, I then placed the case in the hands of a solicitor and it finally got a hearing in the Circuit Court in 1995.

It would appear from statistics recently furnished by the EEA that some 30 per cent of women and 5 per cent of men suffer sexual harassment in the workplace at some time or other. One should not infer from those statistics that all the sexual harassment suffered is caused by members of the opposite gender.

This means that many readers of today's newspapers or their close relatives have actual experience of suffering sexual harassment in the past or at present.

If any reader is in the unpleasant position of being sexually harassed at present, she or he is faced with the stark choice of either putting up with the unpleasantness or doing something positive about it.

It is seldom that sexual harassment takes place in front of witnesses. If you find yourself being sexually harassed I would advise you to summon up the courage to tell your union representative, senior management, members of your family, the EEA, etc., what the problem is and, if everything else fails, report it to the police. If you are prepared to report it to the police then you should also be prepared to urgently seek other employment.

Based on my own experience I would recommend that, if you are forced to make a complaint to a more senior member of management, you should make the complaint in writing rather than verbally. This serves two purposes: (a) It tends to concentrate their minds on the matter and convince them that you do not lightly make that allegation and (b) It is more tangible proof that you did make the complaint to management.

If you are in such circumstances, I know that you find it very unpleasant. There is no reason why you should be forced to tolerate it any longer than necessary.

Why not telephone or write to the Chief Executive, Employment Equality Agency, 36 Upper Mount Street, Dublin 2 (Tel.: 01-6605966) and obtain their advice on how best to deal with your problem.

APPENDIX I

CODE OF PRACTICE:
MEASURES TO PROTECT THE DIGNITY OF WOMEN AND MEN AT WORK

FOREWORD BY MINISTER FOR EQUALITY AND LAW REFORM

I very much welcome the publication of this Code of Practice which was developed at my request under the expert guidance of the Employment Equality Agency.

It represents the fruits of constructive co-operation by employer and employee representatives, including IBEC and ICTU, and provides a valuable guide both to employers and workers as to their duties and responsibilities regarding their, and their colleagues', conduct in the workplace.

I hope to be in a position to grant statutory recognition to the Code under forthcoming employment equality legislation but in the meantime I feel it is a valuable document which should be studied by all with a view to creating and maintaining an atmosphere conducive to good working relationships to the ultimate benefit of both workers and the enterprise.

The Programme for Competitiveness and Work recognises the role of the Employment Equality Agency in the promotion, monitoring and review of the Code. I look forward to receipt of the Agency's advice regarding the practical operation of the Code.

Mervyn Taylor
Minister for Equality and Law Reform
September 1994

INTRODUCTION

1.1 This Code of Practice is issued in accordance with the European Commission Recommendation and Code of Practice of 27 November 1991 and the Resolution of the Council of Ministers of 29 May 1990.[1]

1.2 The European Commission Code describes its objective as:
"to encourage the development and implementation of policies and practices which establish working environments free of sexual harassment and in which women and men respect one another's human integrity".

1.3 This Code therefore aims to provide:
— guidance towards creating a work environment free of sexual harassment:
— a framework for dealing effectively with complaints of sexual harassment when they arise.

1.4 It is important that action be taken to deal effectively with sexual harassment in the workplace not only because it is unjust for those who are its direct victims but also because of the indirect negative effects on the working environment generally and the economic costs arising from sick absences, lost productivity and of litigation.

1.5 It is hoped that employers will find this Code of practical use. The recommendations should be applied in a way which is appropriate to the individual employment. In particular, small and medium -sized organisations may need to adapt the procedures recommended.

1.6 When preparing this Code of Practice the Employment Equality Agency consulted with the Irish Business and Employers Confederation, the Irish Congress of Trade unions and other

---

[1] Commission Recommendations and Code of Practice on Protecting the Dignity of Women and Men at Work (OJ No. 49/1, 24.2.92)

appropriate bodies. The agency has taken account of the views expressed by these organisations to the greatest extent possible in preparing this Code.

1.7 Information and advice on sexual harassment procedures is available to employers, employees and their representative organisations, in confidence, from the Employment Equality Agency.

2. Defining Sexual Harassment

2.1 In both the Resolution of the Council of Minister (29 May 1990) and European Commission Code of Practice, sexual harassment is defined as

"unwanted conduct of a sexual nature or other conduct based on sex affecting the dignity of women and men at work."

2.2 It is the unwanted nature of sexual harassment which distinguishes it from behaviour which is welcome and reciprocal.

2.3 Sexual harassment is often misrepresented as sexually motivated behaviour; experience shows, however, that it results primarily from abuse of power.[2] This is one of the reasons why this type of behaviour is so frequently experienced by employees who are junior to the perpetrator in the employment power structure, although employee—employee harassment is also common.

2.4. Examples of some forms of sexual harassment are listed below:
  (i) *Non—verbal/visual sexual harassment*
  — sexually suggestive or pornographic pictures and calendars
  — leering, offensive, whistling.
  (ii) *Verbal sexual harassment*
  — unwelcome sexual advances

---

[2] Michael Rubenstein's Report, *The Dignity of Women at Work*, for the Commission of European Communities supports this view.

— unwelcome pressure for social contact

— sexually suggestive jokes, remarks or innuendo.

(iii) *Physical sexual harassment*

— unwelcome physical contact such as groping, pinching, patting or unnecessary touching.

— unwelcome fondling or kissing.

— sexual assault or rape.[3]

2.5 Sexual harassment may impact on an employee by creating an intimidating, hostile or humiliating working environment. Alternatively, and employee's response to sexual harassment may be used, implicitly or explicitly, as a basis for employment decisions affecting that employee.[4]

2.6 To facilitate identifying sexual harassment in employment, it should be noted that:

— sexual harassment may occur outside the workplace, e.g. in a hotel, a person's home, a car, or on the street; the degree of control available to the employer in the particular circumstances would be a relevant factor;

— the perpetrator of sexual harassment need not necessarily be senior to the recipient by may be at the same level in the organisation, a junior colleague or a non—employee (e.g. a client, customer or supplier);

— sexual harassment of men by women or same sex harassment may occur.

2.7 As emphasised by the European Commission Code of Practice, the right to be treated with dignity in employment is and individual right; thus each employee should be free to determine what behaviour is acceptable to her/him. This right should not be undermined by the fact that the perpetrator, or indeed other colleagues, may consider the offending behaviour acceptable.

---

[3] Other civil/criminal proceedings may also be appropriate.

[4] Council Resolution on the Protection of the Dignity of Women at Work (OJ No. C157, 27.6.90).

3. The Law and Employer's Responsibilities

3.1 In 1985 the Labour Court, relying on the Employment Equality Act, 1977, stated that [5]

"freedom from sexual harassment is a condition of work which and employee of either sex is entitled to expect. The Court will accordingly treat any denial of that freedom as discrimination within the terms of the Employment Equality Act, 1977."

It should be noted that the protection of the 1977 Act also extends to vocational training.

3.2 Sexual harassment in employment may contravene the 1977 Act if it is unwelcome and offensive to the recipient, and the perpetrator knew or ought reasonably to have known that the conduct complained of was unwelcome and offensive to the recipient. An employer may, in certain circumstances, be liable for such conduct.

3.3 Employers have a duty to seek to ensure that the working environment is free of sexual harassment. Thus, in sex discrimination cases alleging sexual harassment the case is brought against the employer and not the perpetrator.

3.4 In order to deal with the problem of sexual harassment in employment, employers should develop strategies aimed at prevention and accessible complaints procedures. Experience has shown that such measures are most effective when integrated into broader equal opportunities policies.

3.5 Employers should note that, depending on the circumstances of the particular case, the Labour Court may take into consideration, when assessing and employer's liability for discrimination, the fact that an employer has implemented a code of practice to counteract sexual harassment in the workplace.

---

[5] Labour Court Order EEO 2/85, paragraph 10.

3.6 It is important for employers to bear in mind that determining whether sexual harassment is unlawful in particular circumstances is a matter not for employers but for the courts. However, employers have a powerful role to play in preventing unlawful and/or unacceptable standards of behaviour in the workplace.

4. Prevention

4.1 Employers should issue a policy statement expressing the employer's commitment to providing a working environment free of sexual harassment.

4.2 A policy on sexual harassment in employment is most effective when the chief executive is committed to its implementation and ensures that management and supervisors are informed as to their duties under it and are adequately trained to carry out those duties.

4.3 The development of policies on sexual harassment may be carried out in consultation with employees or their representatives, as appropriate.

4.4 It is recommended that policy statements should —

- (i) define inappropriate behaviours in employment which may constitute sexual harassment and advise that such behaviours may in certain circumstances be unlawful;

- (ii) state that sexual harassment will be considered to be a disciplinary offence and subject to normal disciplinary sanctions;

- (iii) state clearly that employees have a right to a working environment free of sexual harassment;

- (iv) state that all managers and supervisors will be required to implement the policy and to set appropriate standards of behaviour by their own example;

- (v) state that employees will be required to comply with the policy;

(vi) explain clearly the procedures to be followed if an employee wishes to make a complaint about sexual harassment;

(vii) state that disciplinary action will be taken against the perpetrator if sexual harassment is found to have occurred;

(viii) state that the victimisation of a complainant, or of an employee who gives evidence regarding sexual harassment, will be subject to disciplinary action;

(ix) reassure employees that complaints of sexual harassment will be treated with sensitivity and will be treated confidendentially as far as possible;

(x) indicate any counselling/support services available.

4.5 Policy statements should be communicated to all employees and others who may impact on the working environment (for example, customers or suppliers); in particular they should be —
   (a) provided to all new employees;
   (b) circulated from time to time among employees;
   (c) clearly visible in appropriate locations where employees and others will see the statement frequently, for example, in canteens, on office notice boards or in changing rooms.

4.6 It is recommended that training on sexual harassment be part of general training programmes for employees so that it is integrated into core training activities.

4.7 Sexual harassment policies should be kept under review to ensure effectiveness.

5. Complaints Procedures

5.1 Employers should provide clear procedures to deal with complaints of sexual harassment promptly and effectively. All procedures should be based on principles of fairness and natural justice, in consultation with trades unions or employee representatives, where appropriate.

5.2 Employees should have access to both informal and formal procedures to deal with sexual harassment problems.

5.3 Advice and assistance regarding sexual harassment and the relevant procedures should be available in confidence to employees experiencing the problem. Any person providing such advice and assistance should receive specialised training. Where practicable, a person of the same sex as the complainant should be available if requested.

5.4 Complaints procedures should be kept under review to ensure effectiveness.

(A) Resolving Problems Informally

5.5 Employees should be advised to attempt to resolve the problem informally if this is possible. The objective of an informal approach is to resolve the difficulty with the minimum of conflict. Employees should be advised to explain clearly to the perpetrator that the behaviour in question is unwelcome and offensive; it may be the case that the perpetrator does not realise the effect of the behaviour on the complainant.

5.6 Where employees would find it difficult or embarrassing to communicate directly with the perpetrator, they should be advised to communicate through a third party, for example, a friend, sympathetic colleague, line supervisor/manager, or union representative.

(B) Formal Procedures

5.7 If the problem continues or if it is not appropriate to resolve the problem informally(for example, because of the severity of the harassment) it will be necessary to use the formal complaints procedures. It is recommended that formal procedures should —

(i)   state clearly the procedure to be followed when making a complaint and to whom a complaint should be made, usually the line supervisor/ manager will be the appropriate person. However, where this is not suitable and alternative should be provided to bypass the line supervisor/manager;

(ii) encourage both parties to seek appropriate advice/ representation at an early stage;

(iii) provide that complaints be investigated, where practicable, by at least two individuals who have received appropriate training to enable them to pursue the investigation in a sensitive and objective manner. The advice/assistance of an outside expert should be available to the investigator(s) if necessary;

(iv) provide that, where practicable, at least one of the persons investigating the complaint will be of the same sex as the complainant it s/he requests this;

(v) provide that the investigation will be pursued with due respect for the rights of both the complainant and the alleged harasser;

(vi) provide that the complaint will be investigated confidentially as far as possible;

(vii) provide that the investigation will be carried out with the minimum of delay consistent with fairness to both parties;

(viii) provide that both parties may be accompanies/represented at interviews held during the investigation.

(ix) provide that the investigator(s) keep a record of all inter views/meeting held during the investigation;

(x) provide for a range of penalties corresponding to the severity of the harassment;

(xi) provide that where transfer of one of the parties is appropriate, the complainant will not be transferred unless s/he requests transfer;

(xii) provide penalties for victimisation of either a complainant or witness;

(xiii) provide of an appeal mechanism, if it is concluded that sexual harassment has occurred.

5.8 It should be noted that where a complaint is not upheld by the formal investigation, this does not necessarily indicate that the complaint was malicious. While a malicious complaint will generally be treated as misconduct under the disciplinary procedure, the application of this provision should not be such as to deter employees from bringing forward legitimate complaints.

5.9 The recommendations on procedures should be adapted to suit the structure and size of individual employments. Existing grievance procedures should be varied as appropriate.

5.10 Managers/supervisors should carefully monitor the workplace following a complaint which is held to be well founded, with particular reference to the offender's behaviour and the prevention of victimisation of the complainant. If further harassment is noted, action should be taken by the employer to bring it to an end.

6. Trades Unions and Employees

6.1 Sexual harassment is an issue for trades unions, both as employers and employee representatives. Trades unions have a responsibility to try to ensure that the working environment is free of sexual harassment. It is recommended that trades unions should:

(i)   have clear policy statements on sexual harassment;

(ii) co-operate with employers in the development and review of appropriate policies and procedures in the workplace;

(iii) include appropriate clauses in agreements in the context of the collective bargaining process;

(iv) raise awareness about sexual harassment problems and how to deal with them through education, information and training;

(v) ensure that union activists/officials set acceptable standards of behaviour by their own example;

(vi) ensure that union representatives respond to complaints of this kind in a sensitive and supportive way;

(vii) ensure that officials receive adequate training to enable them to respond effectively to sexual harassment problems and to advise members of legal rights and time limits;

(viii) encourage members to seek help if they are experiencing sexual harassment;

(ix) encourage members to support colleagues experiencing sexual harassment;

(x) ensure victimisation, either by colleagues or management, does not occur;

(xi) ensure that where both the complainant and the accused harasser are represented by the same union, both representatives are at the same level in the union;

(xii) ensure that, where practicable, representation is by a person of the same sex if requested.

6.2 All employees have a role in creating the working environment in which they work. Employees can discourage unacceptable standards of behaviour by the example of their own behaviour and by being supportive of colleagues experiencing sexual harassment.

6.3 Employees subjected to sexual harassment in employment should:

(i) communicate clearly to the harasser, either directly or through a third party, that the conduct in question is unwelcome and offensive;

(ii) seek advice and assistance if the conduct continues and make a formal complaint if appropriate;

(iii) keep a record of the conduct complained of.

7. Review

7.1 It is only when the Code of Practice is in operation that short-comings may become apparent. It is important, therefore, that it is subject to periodic review. The Employment Equality Agency will review the operation of the Code at regular intervals and advise the Minister for Equality and Law Reform of any changes which may by necessary or desirable.

APPENDIX II

SAMPLE SEXUAL HARASSMENT POLICIES

This Appendix contains two sample policies. The first is relatively comprehensive and seeks to contextualise the company's policy on sexual harassment in the light of its general policy on employment equality. A company may, however, choose to circulate some of the information in the form of guidelines. Alternatively, it may opt to shorten the policy by eliminating the general information on employment equality policy and focusing entirely on sexual harassment. The second sample policy, which could also be issued as an internal memo, is simply intended to cover a number of essential points, highlighting the most important issues.

The policies in question are provided for illustration purposes. They should be amended in order to suit local conditions in any company in which they are implemented. Material can, and often should, be added, deleted or modified as appropriate.

Sample policies are also available from the Employment Equality Agency, the Irish Business and Employers Confederation and the Irish Congress of Trade Unions. The addresses and telephone numbers of these and other relevant organisations are contained in Appendix III.

SAMPLE 1: LONG POLICY

1. Policy Statement

Murphy Ltd. is an equal opportunities employer and is committed to promoting equal opportunities in the company. All employees are asked to co-operate with the company in order to create an equal opportunities working environment. In that context, Murphy Ltd. appreciates the support of all its employees in creating and sustaining a working environment which is free from sexual harassment and which respects the contribution made by each

individual employee. In line with Harvey Ltd.'s general policy on employment equality, sexual harassment is regarded as being completely unacceptable conduct which will not be tolerated. Any employee found to have sexually harassed a colleague, client or any other party will be subject to disciplinary
action.

2. Equal Opportunity

All employees of the company will be treated on the basis of their abilities and merits and according to the requirements of the job. Each and every employee will have equal opportunity to advance within the company and have equal access to all training opportunities within the organisation. The company does not discriminate against any employee or applicant for a position within the company on the basis of his or her sex and/or marital status in terms of recruitment, remuneration and conditions of work, training and work experience and opportunities for career development and promotion.

3. What Is Sexual Harassment?

Sexual harassment is discriminatory behaviour which is sexual in nature and is unwelcomed and unreciprocated by the victim. The Department of Equality and Law Reform's Code of Practice on sexual harassment lists all of the following as examples of sexual harassment:

- hanging sexually suggestive or pornographic pictures and calendars;
- leering, offensive gestures, whistling;
- unwelcome sexual advances;
- unwelcome pressure for social contact;
- sexually suggestive jokes, remarks or innuendo;
- unwelcome physical contact such as groping, pinching, patting or unnecessary touching;
- unwelcome fondling or kissing;
- sexual assault or rape.

Such conduct on the part of employees is not in anyone's interests. It is damaging both to employees and to the company and it will not, for that reason, be tolerated by Murphy Ltd.

4. The Responsibilities of Employees

It is the responsibility of all employees to ensure that sexual harassment does not occur in the organisation. There is a particular responsibility on managers and supervisors, if possible, to prevent the occurrence of incidents of sexual harassment. Supervisors and managers should also make a special effort to limit the potential for sexual harassment to occur.

Supervisors and managers are also responsible for handling complaints. If a complaint is made to a manager or supervisor, he or she should be understanding and sympathetic. The complaint should be taken seriously and, ideally, recorded in writing. If a supervisor or managers receives a complaint, he or she should, where possible, contact the company's equality officer at extension XXX.

5. How to Make a Complaint

Any employee wishing to make a complaint should take the following steps:

First, the person or persons who are responsible for the harassment should be told to stop it, immediately.

Secondly, if the employee does not feel confident in speaking to the alleged harasser, he or she should ask someone one to speak to the harasser. A supervisor, manager or trade union official can be approached for help.

Thirdly, if the harassment does not stop, or alternatively if a person is not comfortable with pursuing the first two options, the individual can make a formal complaint to management. This compliant should be made first to one's immediate supervisor. If the employee is not comfortable, for whatever reason, in making that complaint to his or her immediate supervisor, then it can be addressed to (name of person) in the equal opportunities office.

The complaint can be made orally or in writing. A person making a complaint can be accompanied by another person or persons, including a union representative. Records should be kept at all times. At some point that complaint will be recorded in writing.

6. Action to be Taken when a Complaint is Made

It is the responsibility of every manager and supervisor in the organisation to deal with complaints of sexual harassment. He or she cannot ignore or trivialise the issue. Failure to act can result in disciplinary action. The manager or supervisor should do the following:

- be sympathetic and understanding of the individual making the complaint

- re-assure the individual making the complaint of her rights in this regard

- document, where possible, the complaint

As a course of action, the manager or supervisor may attempt either:

a. In situations where the allegation of harassment is not serious, and subject to the wishes of the person making the complaint, an approach should be made to the person or person(s) alleged to have done the harassing. They should be requested to stop. It is the supervisor's or manager's responsibility to ensure that the behaviour is stopped.

b. Where serious allegations of harassment are made, the manager or supervisor should interview the person or persons alleged to have done the harassing and detailed statement(s) should be obtained.

Regardless of which approach the supervisor or manager takes, he or she should be aware of two factors:

First, all complaints have to be handled in a professional and caring manner. Confidentiality, where possible, should be maintained.

Secondly, the equal opportunities office will provide advice and assistance to all employees. A manager or supervisor, on receipt of a complaint, is advised to use the support of the Equal Opportunities Office. This is the particularly the case for more serious allegations of sexual harassment. If a supervisor or manager, for whatever reason, is unwilling to deal with a complaint of sexual harassment, he or she should inform the equal opportunities office who will then handle the complaint.

7. Rights of the Parties

Complaints will be dealt with seriously. An employee is free to make a complaint. He or she will not be victimised for making a complaint. For example, no promotional or training opportunity will be denied. However, if a complaint is found to be unwarranted or malicious, disciplinary action may be taken.

The person who is alleged to have done the harassing has rights. He or she is entitled to representation, a fair and impartial hearing, and the right to challenge a claim. An allegation of sexual harassment remains an allegation until such an investigation finds it to be sexual harassment.

8. Penalties

Disciplinary action may be taken against an employee if after an investigation the allegation is upheld. Penalties are in accordance with the normal disciplinary procedure set out in the employee's handbook. Disciplinary action may also include transfer of an employee who is found to have harassed another employee.

9. Summary

Sexual harassment is sex discrimination. It demeans and damages people. Murphy Ltd. is committed to providing an environment which is free of harassment and which values the contribution of all employees. The company recognises that the issue of whether sexual harassment has occurred requires a factual determination based on all the evidence received. The Company also recognises that false accusations of sexual harassment can have serious effects on innocent men and women. We trust that all employees will continue to act in a responsible and professional manner to establish a pleasant working environment free of harassment.

SAMPLE 2: SHORT POLICY

A Policy on Sexual Harassment

Note: This is short policy on sexual harassment, written in the form of a memo to employees

To: All Employees

Re: Policy on Sexual Harassment

Sexual harassment is illegal and against the policies of [name of company]. Sexual harassment involves (a) making unwelcome sexual advances or requests for sexual favours or other verbal or physical conduct of a sexual nature a conditions of employment, or (b) making submission to or rejection of such conduct the basis for employment decisions, or (c) creating an intimidating, offensive, or hostile working environment by such conduct.

The following are examples of sexual harassment:

- Verbal: Sexual innuendo, suggestive comments, insults, threats, jokes about gender-specific traits, or sexual propositions;

- Visual: Making suggestive or insulting noises, leering, whistling, or making obscene gestures; and

- Physical: Touching, pinching, brushing the body, coercing sexual intercourse, or assault.

Any employee who believes he or she has been the subject of sexual harassment should report the alleged conduct immediately to his or her immediate supervisor or to Mr. X or Ms. Y in the Personnel Department. A confidential investigation of any complaint will be undertaken immediately.

Any employee found by the company to have sexually harassed another employee will be subject to appropriate disciplinary sanctions ranging from a written warning up to and including dismissal. Retaliating or discriminating against an employee for complaining about sexual harassment is prohibited.

APPENDIX III

USEFUL ADDRESSES

Chartered Institute of Arbitrators (Irish Branch)
42 Thormanby Road, Howth, Co. Dublin
Tel.: 01-8394077

Council for the Status of Women
64 Lower Mount Street, Dublin 2
Tel.: 01-615268

Department of Equality and Law Reform
43-49 Mespil Road, Dublin 4
Tel.: 01-6670344

Employment Appeals Tribunal
Davitt House, 65a Adelaide Road
Dublin 2
Tel.: 01-6765861

Employment Equality Agency
36 Upper Mount Street
Dublin 2
Tel.: 01-6605966   4/7 3333

Irish Business and Employers Confederation
Baggot Bridge House, 84 Lower Baggot Street
Dublin 2
Tel.: 01-6601011   6051 500

Irish Congress of Trade Unions
Head Office, 19 Raglan Road
Dublin 4
Tel.: 01-6680641

Irish Small and Medium Enterprises Association
32 Kildare Street, Dublin 2
Tel.: 01-6622755

Labour Court
Tom Johnson House
Haddington Road
Dublin 4
Tel.: 01-6608444

Labour Relations Commission
Tom Johnson House, Haddington Road
Dublin 4
Tel.: 01-6608444

Mediators Institute of Ireland
13 Royal Terrace West
Dun Laoghaire, Co. Dublin
Tel.: 01-2845277

Rape Crisis Centre
70 Lower Leeson Street
Dublin 2
Tel.: 01-6614911 (Consulting Service)
01-6614564 (after 5.30p.m. and weekends)
1800-778888 (freefone)

UK Equal Opportunities Commission
Overseas House, Quay Street,
Manchester M3 3HN, England
Tel.: 061-8339244

Women Against Sexual Harassment
312 The Chandlery
50 Westminster Bridge Road
London SE1 7QY, England
Tel.: 071-7217592

TABLE OF CASES

TABLE OF STATUTES

INDEX